money sucks

a memoir on why too much or too little can ruin you

Michael Baughman

Skyhorse Publishing

Skyhorse Publishing books may be purchased in bulk at special discounts for sales promotion, corporate gifts, fund-raising, or educational purposes. Special editions can also be created to specifications. For details, contact the Special Sales Department, Skyhorse Publishing, 307 West 36th Street, 11th Floor, New York, NY 10018 or info@skyhorsepublishing.com.

Visit our website at www.skyhorsepublishing.com.

10 9 8 7 6 5 4 3 2 1

Library of Congress Cataloging-in-Publication Data is available on file.

Cover design by Danielle Ceccolini

Cover photo credit Thinkstock.com

ISBN: 978-1-62873-629-8

eISBN: 978-1-62873-986-2

Printed in the United States of America

This book is dedicated to everyone it offends.

I

feeding the wolf

Something is profoundly wrong with the way we live today. For thirty years we have made a virtue out of the pursuit of material self-interest: indeed, this very pursuit now constitutes whatever remains of our sense of collective purpose. We know what things cost but have no idea what they are worth.

—Tony Judt, *Ill Fares the Land*

The worship of the golden calf has found a new and heartless image in the cult of money and the dictatorship of an economy which is faceless and lacking any true human goal.

—Pope Francis

nickled and dimed

Throughout my adult life, my income has fallen within a couple of thousand dollars of the national median income. My wife, Hilde, has been kind enough to oversee our financial affairs, so for fifty years I've had little idea how much money I made per week, month, or year. Whatever it was seemed enough, even a little more than enough, so everything was fine.

In the years before Hilde, as an only child in western Pennsylvania and then Hawaii, my father's business career kept my mother and me in relative comfort. I have a single lasting memory concerning money from the Pennsylvania years. On a warm summer day, we were visiting my grandparents in Jeanette, an industrial town near Pittsburgh, and all of us—father, mother, grandparents, aunt, uncle, and three cousins—had gathered on the front porch after dinner.

"Hey, Mikey!" my father said in his customarily loud voice. "Here's a riddle for you!" A wide smile on his ruddy face, he held both big hands toward me, palms upward, a shiny silver coin in each hand. I was so young I had no idea what the coins were, though one was nearly twice the size of the other. "Take whichever one you want!" he demanded.

Sensing a trick, I reached and took the smaller coin.

"Look!" my father exclaimed in a voice that must have been heard up and down the block. "Look what Mikey did! He grabbed the dime instead of the nickel! When this kid grows up, he'll be rich!"

At that precise moment, I became resentful of people who place money at the center of their lives.

When I was ten years old, we moved all the way from western Pennsylvania to Hawaii, where I attended Punahou School in Honolulu, the same prep school Barack Obama graduated from in 1979, and which, in his autobiography, he accurately defined as "an incubator for the island's elite."

After my Punahou graduation in 1955, my parents moved to California, and for the next few years I led a chaotic life: as a college football player, a laborer, a sometimes homeless vagabond, and an enlisted man in the army in Germany, where I met and married Hilde. Three years after my army discharge, with a master's degree in English Language Arts from San Francisco State, I took a college teaching job in Ashland, Oregon, where Hilde and I, along with our extended family, live today.

Ashland, thanks to its Shakespeare Festival, university, ski resort and magnificent surrounding countryside, has often been included in those Ten Best Small Towns and Ten Best Places to Retire lists published in national magazines. The resulting notoriety has made it a relatively expensive place, with neighborhoods of luxury cars and monstrous SUVs parked alongside multi-million-dollar homes. A surprising number of these dwellings are 4,000, 6,000, 8,000 square feet, with a few even larger than that. Many of these lavish residences are occupied by retired elderly couples rattling through their golden years among six or eight bathrooms, ten or a dozen bedrooms, plus maybe an indoor pool, billiard room, and arboretum.

Luckily, Hilde and I arrived in town decades before gentrification set in, so our modest income remains more than adequate. We've even been able to help our children with modest sums of money when they needed it. Our daughter, Ingrid, is a fifth grade teacher who loves her work and does it very well, and our son, Pete, who read Thoreau and took his ideas to heart, is happy with a hard, simple outdoor life, working as an arborist and specializing in big tree work.

I include these details to make an essential point: my life has thrown me into close contact with people in every economic circumstance, from the homeless to the very rich indeed. I've slept on the ground in Central Park in wintertime New York as well as in exquisitely furnished mansions in Hawaii. I've dined on gourmet food at private clubs and gone three days and nights without a bite to eat.

All of this matters because of our oldest grandchild, Billy Hansen, Ingrid's son, who became a college freshman this year. Before it was time for him to leave home, I felt obliged to talk to him about what I believe to be a healthy attitude toward money. In attempting this, I knew I had to be careful. An overbearing adult will usually do more harm than good when dealing with a youngster, and a condescending adult will do worse. No matter how clear things seemed to me, I had no right to assume that someone else, who happens to be younger, who I happen to love, should embrace my viewpoints. But I did want Billy to know what I believed: that money is a necessary evil, and that he needed to figure out how evil it was, and how much of it was necessary.

While preparing to write this narrative about the months between Billy's commitment to Regis University and his departure for Denver, I made notes at least once a day. The places, events and conversations, my random thoughts, my mistakes, my confusions and biases, are accurately recorded.

To begin with, some admissions: I feel nothing but disdain for today's Republican Party, and I regard many rich people with a blend composed of equal parts scorn and pity. When Billy and I talked, I usually tried to hide these biases, or at the very least to soften them. But occasionally I slipped up and found myself trashing the Republicans and the rich. All I can offer in defense of my failings is what seems to me to be the clear truth: Republicans have been trashing America lately, and history leads to the inescapable conclusion that the rich, in their sundry ways, have been trashing the poor for centuries, and they remain hard at it today.

Timing had a lot to do with my dilemma. Adding to my lifelong skepticism about the actual value of money, and my horror at what too much or too little of it can do to decent people, was the 2012 presidential campaign. Choosing from among a pack of hacks and fools, the Republicans nominated Wilfred Mitt Romney, a wealthy man, as Hunter Thompson once expressed it in regard to another Republican (Richard Nixon), "with no soul, no inner convictions, with the integrity of a hyena and the style of a poison toad."

Republican lies and evasions proliferated through the months before Billy left home, and this was the year he would vote for the first time in a state that mattered. Was my grandson ready for Mitt Romney? I hoped not. Was he ready for me? Maybe.

Quotations from books, plays, poems, and magazines are liberally interspersed through my narrative. Many of these come from writers who have influenced me from an early age, and despite the fact that twenty-first-century technology seems to be working relentlessly to deaden us to the written word in all its traditional forms, I cling to a hope that my grandson and his generation, and generations to follow, will somehow learn to take some time and find quiet places to sit and read.

$ $ $

Even in a palace it is possible to live well.

—Roman Emperor Marcus Aurelius

bigger and better

As one digs deeper into the national character of the Americans, one sees that they have sought the value of everything in this world only in the answer to this single question: how much money will it bring in?

—Alexis de Tocqueville, *Democracy in America*

$ $ $

On a Sunday evening in the lobby of the Ashland High School gym, with friends, coaches, family, and newspaper reporters in attendance, Billy Hansen formally signed his national letter of intent, officially accepting a full-ride scholarship offer to play basketball for Regis University, a private Jesuit school in Denver.

Here is what I had found earlier that day on the school's website:

> Regis University educates men and women of all ages to take leadership roles and to make a positive impact in a changing society . . . This vision challenges us to attain the inner freedom to make intelligent choices. We seek to provide value-centered undergraduate and graduate education, as well as to strengthen commitment to community service. We nurture the life of the mind and the pursuit of truth within an environment conducive to effective teaching, learning and personal development.

Through the years I've recommended books to Billy, and when he was fourteen I thought he was ready for *The Catcher in the Rye*. As I read from the Regis website I remembered Pencey Prep, the fictional school in Agerstown, Pennsylvania that Holden Caulfield attends in the novel.

I read over the passage where Holden tells us that Pencey advertises "in about a thousand magazines" and that their promotional material makes the claim that since 1888 Pencey has been "molding boys into splendid, clear-thinking young men." Included with these ads is a photo of "some hot-shot guy on a horse jumping over a fence." But Holden also tells us that he's never seen a horse anywhere near Pencey, and that he "didn't know anybody there that was splendid and clear-thinking and all. Maybe two guys . . . And they probably came to Pencey that way."

I had both fears and hopes regarding Regis, founded in 1877, eleven years before the fictional Pencey. Hopefully Billy's chosen school wouldn't turn out to be an administrator-bloated, adjunct-taught, grade-inflated, beer-drenched, drug-addled country club for spoiled kids. I wanted to believe that a healthy number of teachers there took the university's stated mission seriously; and I was certain that, as at Pencey, what Regis students brought to their school went a long way toward determining what they would take away.

$ $ $

A winner in the genetic lottery, Billy has been a gifted basketball and baseball player ever since elementary school. Through middle school and high school, he was what teachers and parents commonly call a great kid: an athlete who cultivated friendships outside the jock circle, didn't drink or use drugs, never bragged or swaggered, and took his studies seriously. He was a handsome, popular, justifiably confident boy.

But like nearly all his peers, he seems addicted to cell phones, iPods, video games, and the like. As he grows toward young manhood, with the customary technological and human distractions, he reads less and less. And I've known for two years that he's harbored fantasies about getting rich. The first indication came one afternoon in the high school gym when I overheard him confide to a friend that he hoped to someday live in a mansion.

I can't blame him for that or any other such desires because he's growing up in America, where most people spend a great deal of time discussing, almost always adoringly, often reverently, money and all the presumably wonderful things it can buy, and where everything bigger, from a pizza to a car to a house to a penis, is supposedly better for sure.

I planned to talk about much of this with Billy, and I thought it might possibly work. Besides being relatives, we're friends. Growing up next door to us, he spent countless nights at our house, ate hundreds of meals here, and watched sporting events, TV shows, and movies in our living room. (The TV shows began with *Sponge Bob Squarepants* and *Looney Tunes* and progressed through the years to *House M.D.*) He and I shot thousands of baskets out in the driveway. We hiked, camped, and fished together. We played dozens of games of checkers and chess and hundreds of hands of gin rummy and Texas hold 'em poker. All of this became especially important after his parents divorced and our home became a sanctuary for him when he needed it.

We talk openly and honestly with one another, and it helps that the time I spent in locker rooms and army barracks left me comfortably fluent in the language teenage boys inevitably hear and use.

Naturally enough, these days Billy spends more time out with his friends than he used to, often out of town or out of state for basketball and baseball games; but even then we stay in touch through the same technology I've come to have doubts about: cell phone calls, texting, and Facebook posts.

I felt I had to try to get through to him, and I thought I had a chance.

a parcel of dropsies

A grandfather told his grandson that two wolves inside the boy were fighting. One animal represented peace, love, and kindness, while the other stood for fear, hatred, and greed. "Which one will win?" asked the boy. "Whichever one I feed," answered the grandfather.

—Mohawk Indian lore

The love of possessions is a disease in them.

—Chief Sitting Bull, speaking of Americans at the Powder River Conference, 1877

$ $ $

Billy and I met at the high school gym after his last class to shoot baskets: three-pointers, mid-range jump shots, free throws, and after that some dribbling and cutting drills.

This was baseball season, but practice wouldn't start until half past five, and, insofar as he can, Billy keeps both sports going straight through the year.

The gym was empty, the collapsible bleachers rolled back against the sidewalls. A few decades ago, I played the sport myself, and I still like a basketball court: the bright overhead lights, the smoothly polished floor marked with straight lines, the sounds of a ball bouncing off hardwood and swishing through a clean, white net.

Immediately we fell into the easy rhythm of it, and Billy, a six-foot-three shooting guard, was on. I fed him the ball with bounce passes. The three-pointers and jumpers dropped, and he was hitting fifteen to twenty free throws in a row.

I bounced the ball back after a free throw.

"How're classes going these days?"

"Real good, I think."

"Grades okay?"

Another free throw, another bounce pass back.

"I think so. Yeah, they're good. I have a math test Wednesday."

"Is math still pretty easy for you?"

"Yeah it is."

Another make, another pass, and so it continued.

"It was for me too. I thought about majoring in it."

"How come you didn't?"

"I just liked writing better. I might major in math if I had it to do over. What I mean is, finding jobs you really wanted was easier when I was young. Math's definitely in high demand these days. You have plenty of time to figure out what you like, what you really want to do. However you make a living, you want it to be something you enjoy. Something you care about."

"Philosophy's pretty cool."

"You like philosophy a lot?"

Another make, another pass, and then a pretty girl with dark, lustrous hair walked through a side door into the gym, all the way across the floor and out a door on the far side. When Billy looked back over his shoulder to smile at her, she waved and smiled back.

"Was it a class that got you interested in philosophy?"

"More like a teacher. Actually I was pretty sure I'd hate the class at first, but Mr. Cate made it really interesting. I ended up liking it a lot. Maybe I could figure out a major combining philosophy and math."

After a miss off the back rim, Billy muttered "shit" under his breath and went back to the three-point line.

"If there's time, let's get some tacos after this," I said.

We always ended Billy's shooting sessions with what we called his "routine," meaning that before quitting, he had to hit four three-pointers, four jump shots, and four free throws—twelve consecutive shots without a miss. Today he did it on his third try.

He finished up with ten minutes of the dribbling and cutting drills.

$ $ $

La Tapatia is a typical Mexican combination grocery store and restaurant in Phoenix, a small town a few miles north of Ashland, and on Mondays their tacos, remarkably good ones, sell for a dollar apiece.

Everything in the old building is immaculate. Entering from a busy two-lane street, you pass by shelves stacked with canned goods, jars of cookies and candy, small sacks of tortilla flour, and dried peppers and beans, and then come to a long counter with meat displayed behind glass: whole fish laid out on crushed ice, prawns on ice, strips of lean beef, chorizo sausage, tongue, lung, brains, gobs of assorted intestines packed into plastic bags, and deep fried pork rinds. Where the display case ends, the restaurant begins with a wooden counter where orders are taken and numbers are handed out.

A prominent poster is taped to the wall beside the ordering counter:

THE LA TAPATIA CHALLENGE
BUY 30 TACOS FOR $30

EAT THE 30 TACOS IN 30 MINUTES
GET YOUR $30 BACK AND WIN A $50 PRIZE

"A guy on the water polo team tried it last week," Billy told me, indicating the poster. "He got up to twenty-two and had to sprint outside and puke. We heard a while back some guy from Medford made it up to twenty-eight-and-a-half. I'd like to see Joey Chestnut try it."

"He's the one who beat Kobayashi in the hot dog eating contest."

"Right."

Billy ordered five marinated pork tacos with horchata—an iced milk, sugar, and cinnamon drink—and I decided on three beefsteak and two marinated pork with a Negra Modelo beer.

We took a small table between two big tables crowded with young men, at least half of them Mexican, apparently manual laborers, all of them wearing T-shirts, work pants, and dusty boots. They talked and laughed while they waited for their food, most of them with bottles of Mexican beer in front of them.

Billy brought us small bowls of medium hot salsa, marinated carrots, and plastic forks from the counter in front of the kitchen.

As usual, the TV set high on a shelf against the back wall was on, without sound. At lunchtime the set often showed either *Looney Tunes* cartoons or a Mexican soap opera, occasionally a soccer game, but now, later in the day, the content level had been lowered by several notches. It appeared to be some sort of Fox News political panel show.

When given a choice between watching something and watching nothing, most modern Americans will watch something, no matter what it is. While Billy and I sipped our drinks and made small talk, we kept glancing up at the screen.

A close-up of John Boehner's orange face appeared.

Next came Carl Rove, complete with shiny dome, sagging jowls, and multiple chins.

Donald Trump followed Rove, to be quickly replaced by Rush Limbaugh.

Billy and I had watched *King Henry IV, Part One* together at the Shakespeare Festival's outdoor theater, and ever since, whenever I see Limbaugh, I immediately think of what Prince Hal called Falstaff: a "swollen parcel of dropsies."

After ten seconds of the swollen parcel, it was Bill O'Reilly's turn, and, reverting to an adolescent state of mind, as I sometimes do, I fantasized about facing O'Reilly in a mixed martial arts cage match.

"You don't like those guys, do you?" Billy asked me.

"How can you tell?"

"The look on your face."

I should have kept my mouth shut but didn't. "The thing is, they're bullshit artists," I said. "They tell self-serving lies.

The television people tell lies to help the politicians. The politicians tell lies to help rich people make more money than they already have, and the rich people pay them all back one way or another. That's what it boils down to. It's complicated but you'll find out about it soon enough. One thing the bullshit artists do, they're doing it now in politics, is argue that poor people are parasites, that they sponge off the rich. But the truth is more the other way around. A hell of a lot of rich people sponge off the work poor people do."

"So you think it's all about money?" he said.

"Mostly," I said. "Or it could be a little more complicated than that. Maybe money replaces something people wish they had but couldn't ever get. Some of those guys, maybe even most of them, maybe they wanted to be athletes, or over six feet tall, or popular with pretty girls, or outstanding students—something, who knows what—but they more or less sucked at everything."

A young Mexican man at a neighboring table pointed up at Rove, back on camera now. "Who's that one?" he asked the gringo friend sitting beside him.

"El scumbago," the young man answered with a smile.

Our tacos arrived, and Billy asked a reasonable question.

"How much money do you think a person actually needs? I mean, to live on for, say, a year?"

"It depends on a lot—where you live, how big your family is. It gets more expensive all the time everywhere but some places are a lot worse than others. San Francisco, New York, Honolulu, places like that cost a lot. Even Ashland these days is bad enough. Nobody wants to be truly poor anywhere, that's awful, it's horrible. I've done it. But most people want way more money than they need. And a few people actually want less. An author who came through town last week wrote a book about a guy named Dan—I forget the last name—who got so sick of the whole mess that he gave up money completely. *The Man Who Quit Money* is the title of the book. Dan claims he's perfectly happy, he has friends, thinks a lot—philosophizes—and somehow figures out satisfying ways to pass his time. He sleeps in caves—this is somewhere in Utah—and lives on wild plants, road kill, and food he gets out of dumpsters. It definitely sounds extreme but he claims he's content that way. He loves the country there. Living in a place you really want to live in is important, no doubt about that."

"Road kill?"

"You know, animals that get run over—deer and raccoons I guess. Possums maybe, if they have possums in Utah. Hopefully not skunks. It's extreme but apparently he thought it all out before he did it and he swears he's satisfied. I wouldn't recommend it though."

"No thanks on raccoon tacos. How much money do you and Oma make?"

"We live on about fifty thousand a year. It's more than we need."

Now Donald Trump was back, first scowling about something, then bursting into red-faced laughter.

"See that guy up there?" I said to Billy.

He looked at the screen, just as Trump's laugh turned back into a scowl.

"He's rich," I said, "but I'd be willing to bet Dan in his Utah caves is a happier man."

We worked through our tacos.

Just as we got up from the table, the TV screen showed Newt Gingrich waddling along a city street. "I bet he could make it through thirty tacos," I said.

"He's too fat," Billy answered. "Skinny guys do better in eating contests. Their stomachs aren't surrounded by fat so there's more room for them to expand. That's why Joey Chestnut would have a chance."

$ $ $

> Ezriel had long since learned that the harder people worked, the less they earned.
>
> —Isaac Singer, *The Manor*

sneakers

The day our lives begin to end is the day we are silent about things that matter.

—Martin Luther King Jr.

$ $ $

When I dropped Billy off at the baseball field, I handed over a *Sports Illustrated* article I'd brought along for him to read, a piece that contrasted athletes of the past, namely Muhammad Ali and Olympic sprinters Tommie Smith and John Carlos, with more recent athletes, Michael Jordan and Tiger Woods.

It took an all-white jury only thirty minutes to convict Ali for refusing military service in Vietnam, and he was subsequently sentenced to five years in prison. Though he didn't serve time in jail, he lost what almost surely would have been the three most lucrative years of his career. When they raised their fists in the black power salute on the podium at Mexico City in 1968, Smith and Carlos brought years of ferocious retribution down on themselves. In contrast, neither Jordan nor Woods—who each have far more money than any hundred humans could possibly need—has ever taken a public stance on any moral or social issue, for one simple reason: offending people who deserve it would have cost them some of their useless money. When questioned about his silence on civil rights, Jordan had no apparent qualms about answering: "Republicans buy sneakers too."

Driving home, I felt troubled, confused about the things I wanted to get across to Billy. I had clear memories of my own youth, when I'd seldom accepted guidance offered by adults. Later, in their turn, my own children rarely took my advice seriously unless it happened to suit their immediate purposes. I understood that Billy might not be listening to me all the time, or even very often. He quite likely lived happily with the same instinctive delusion I'd experienced at his age: that youth can somehow conquer anything.

Our daughter's divorce brought further complications. Since splitting up when Billy was seven, Ingrid and her ex husband, Ron, have been responsible parents and thoroughly decent to one another. But Billy and his brother, Jake, divide their time between two different homes and, as I see it, two different worlds. I came to Ashland from 1960s San Francisco to teach college and write. In our free time and ever since, Hilde and I, with our son and daughter in their years with us have immensely enjoyed the southern Oregon outdoors: fly fishing, upland hunting, cross-country skiing, camping, hiking, backpacking, trail-running, mountain-biking, river-rafting.

Ron and his father own a successful jewelry store in Ashland and probably vote Republican. In their free time, they like to play golf. I respect small businesspeople. They take risks and work hard. I've played enough golf to know what a challenging game it is. But I can't ignore what the Republican Party has become in recent years, here in Oregon and everywhere. Ayn Rand greed freaks and Tea Party morons enrage and disgust me. Sometimes I have to bite about half-way through my tongue to keep my mouth shut.

$ $ $

> A man is rich in proportion to the number of things he can afford to let alone.
>
> —Henry Thoreau

> When did I get in the habit of giving these people my soul in exchange for their money?
>
> —Stendhal, *The Red and The Black*

deep in the heart of texans

While our town has a liberal reputation—conservatives often call it the People's Republic of Ashland—Hilde and I live in a distinctly Republican enclave a couple of miles outside the city limits. Nearly all our neighbors have bigger houses and more land than we do. Some of their multi-acre spreads include ponds and swimming pools, with sleek horses grazing over irrigated pastureland.

As is common in rural neighborhoods, everybody gets along reasonably well despite our differences, and groups of us periodically meet for dinner. A few nights after Billy and I enjoyed our tacos at La Tapatia, Hilde and I were guests at the home of a retired couple we refer to as The Texans.

Our two-lane road is about a mile-and-a-half long. We live at one end and the Texans live at the other end, in more ways than one. Mrs. Texas proclaims to anybody who will listen, too loudly and too often, that any American who doesn't have a job is too lazy to work. Mr. Texas repeatedly makes it clear that he fears higher income taxes and increased government intrusion on his life more than anything. So far he has undergone two hip replacements plus prostate surgery, everything, of course, paid for by the government, via Medicare.

Besides political issues, our most conspicuous difference is in our attitudes toward money. Put simply, the Texans believe in accumulating as much and spending as little of it as possible. They are multi-millionaires and dress like paupers—threadbare Goodwill shirts, faded windbreakers, patched pants and dresses, sweatshirts and sweaters with holes worn through the elbows.

Ten years ago, when Ashland passed an insignificant meals tax, they decided they'd never eat at a restaurant in town again. Meals tax or not, they never eat out anywhere unless they have a two-meals-for-the-price-of-one coupon.

There's no law against nudity in Ashland, and four years ago, after a bare-breasted young woman on a skateboard joined the Fourth of July parade, the Texans swore they'd never set foot in town again for anything, and as far as I know they've kept their promise.

One morning two years ago while Hilde and I were jogging, we ran into a young couple walking toward us on the opposite side of the road. The man wore shorts and a T-shirt, and the woman, showing shapely bare breasts, wore only shorts. We smiled and said good morning, and they smiled and said it back. Minutes later we caught up with Mrs. Texas, out for her daily walk and literally quivering with rage. "This place is full of drugged-out hippies!" she sputtered. "And that stupid girl didn't even have big ones!"

Last year at a neighborhood dinner, Mr. Texas gave me a brief summary of his adult life. He attended Reed College—an excellent Portland school said to be one of the most expensive in America—and majored in geology. Though he loved Oregon, he took a job with an oil company in Houston that paid more than he could make here, then soon married Mrs. Texas and settled down. Though they both grew to hate Houston, they remained there through the decades of his working life.

Despite meals taxes, drugged-out hippies, and bare breasts, they had always seemed reasonably content in southern Oregon while Hilde and I had known them. Their primary hobby was a large, well-tended vegetable garden that afforded them lower food costs, as well as fresh air and moderate exercise. Even after canning and freezing, there were always vegetables, melons, and berries left over, which they shared with neighbors, at least partly because they refused to give their surplus to the Food Bank, where freeloaders could get at it. To reciprocate, Hilde gave them cookies, cakes, and candies that come from her sister in Bavaria every year at Christmastime.

We were the first guests to arrive for dinner that night, and Mr. Texas opened the front door for us before we had time to ring the bell. Behind him in the living room, I saw his wife turn the television off. I could tell it was Fox News because I recognized a blond shrew, a regular on the network.

Before Mr. Texas finished mixing our drinks, other guests had arrived, and ten of us spent half an hour making conversation in the living room. I remember every word of a discussion I overheard from a few feet away.

Mrs. Texas grilled a female guest about how much money the woman's daughter made.

"I know your daughter's in television," she said. "She's a newscaster, right?"

"Yes, she is," answered the woman.

"What city is it again?"

"Minneapolis."

"Does she make a lot of money?"

"She's comfortable. She makes enough. She's just fine."

"How much does she make?"

"I'm not really sure just how much she makes."

"Well, *about* how much does she make?"

"Really, I can't say. I just don't know."

"Well, is she rich?"

"I don't really know how much money makes a person rich. Do you?"

"Six million dollars! Six million dollars makes you rich!"

"Well then my daughter's not rich."

"That's too bad!"

A few minutes later, I was standing near the bar with Mr. Texas, listening to him bitterly denounce the federal government for interfering in our lives. When he paused for breath, I baited him with a proposition. "Here's what we should do to get even," I said. "All of us in the neighborhood should get together and refuse our Medicare benefits."

He shook his head and shrugged his shoulders. "Medicare works for me," he said.

Soon after that we sat down to dinner.

During the meal—overcooked beef and excellent vegetables—Mr. Texas announced some surprising news. They had made a quick trip to the "hill country" of southwest Texas and bought a house, at a very low price because of both the economic downturn and the drought afflicting the area, and they had already sold this house, which they had lived in for fifteen years. Their motivation for returning to Texas turned out to be predictably simple: no state or inheritance taxes there.

Two weeks later, the Texans were gone.

A few weeks after they left, we learned from a neighbor what had happened to them once they had settled into their new house.

Their first order of business was to hire low-priced contractors to do extensive remodeling. Due to the heat and the drought, and the near non-existence of topsoil, nothing would grow in their garden. The weather was too hot to go outside in the daytime. They weren't making any friends. Their contractors turned out to be fly-by-nighters and, having been paid in full, disappeared when their work was about halfway done. Mr. Texas decided to finish the job himself. One night Mrs. Texas, on her way to the bathroom, tripped over a tool he'd left in a hallway. She broke her hip, which necessitated replacement surgery, so now they're three for four on government hips.

jocks and brains

The starlings in front of my window continually display their art; they can sound like oriels, quails, corncrakes, even frogs, but they haven't a sound of their own. I call them professors.

—Leo Tolstoy, in a letter

$ $ $

An illogical regard for money wasn't the first serious subject I'd discussed with Billy. While he was still in middle school and already an outstanding athlete, I began talking to him about a cultural conflict I'd first experienced at his age, then later observed.

My youthful athletic abilities had been similar to Billy's, and already as a seventh grader, many people, some of my teachers included, began regarding me, and treating me, as a dumb jock. I should have been bothered by this, but I wasn't. Unfortunately, many jocks, young and old, take a perverse pride in coming across as stupid.

Even in junior high school, a surprising number of my teammates, especially football players, kidded me about reading books and earning decent grades. These boys were proud of barely scraping by in their classes and bragged about the cheating they got away with. This blatant anti-intellectualism—a term I hadn't yet learned at the time—gradually accelerated through my high school years.

In college in Boston on a football scholarship, the anti-intellectualism reached new depths. Though there were exceptions, many players cheated rampantly, joked about cutting classes, and ridiculed any teammate caught studying. They laughed at conscientious students, called bookworms in those days and geeks and nerds today. None of this was entirely the fault of the players. Coaches and upper-class teammates made it abundantly clear to scholarship freshmen that we were at college to play football. Sliding by any way we could in easy classes taught by compliant professors was an integral part of the "program." The head coach, in a pep talk the day before a game, told us with enthusiastic sincerity that we were the only "real men" on campus. He went on to label the general male student population as "lounge lizards and piss ants."

An English professor introduced me to the other side of the equation. I turned in an essay he liked, and he read it aloud to the class. When he handed the paper back, he said he wanted to talk to me after class.

"You write good sentences," he told me in the empty room, "and well organized paragraphs, and you've used them to create an intelligent, persuasive paper. Am I correct in thinking you're a football player?"

"Yes, sir," I said. "Right, I am."

"My advice to you would be to quit."

"Quit?"

"Yes. Quit playing football. The sooner the better."

"Why?"

"Pardon me for being blunt. But why would you or anyone fortunate enough to have been born with a mind want to waste your time rooting around in the mud with violent oafs?"

I tried to argue that not quite all of us were violent by nature, and we weren't all oafs, but I didn't convince him.

Beginning with that experience, I became a fascinated observer of the brain versus jock conflict as it typically operates in America. Years later, after I became a professor myself, I was able to see things from inside the proverbial "ivory tower."

I remember a casual conversation I had at a faculty party with a married couple, an English professor and a history professor. In an unguarded moment, I told them I'd watched my son, an all-state cross-country runner, at a meet that afternoon.

The wife, the English professor, answered abruptly: "Well, we've never gone to an athletic event in our lives—and we never will." The look on her face suggested an offensive odor had wafted into the room.

Because I ran marathons and ultra-marathons, colleagues sometimes half-jokingly called me "crazy." I also fly fished and hunted upland birds, two more strikes against me. Then I became a special contributor to *Sports Illustrated* magazine. Though I wrote mostly about environmental subjects, few of my peers took the work seriously, because it appeared in a national magazine that, in contrast to academic journals, people actually read.

While on assignment in Hawaii to do a piece on the Honolulu Marathon, I spent time with an old surfing buddy. One day while we were hanging out on Waikiki Beach, he told me that he and his friends liked reading my stories in *Sports Illustrated*, and then, when he asked me if I made my living writing, I explained that I also taught at a college.

"You mean you're a professor?" he asked me.

"That's what they call me," I said.

He looked at me with an abject expression I'd have expected after telling him my wife and children had been run over by a log truck. His face showed both shock and dismay, and he clearly felt sorry for me. In the surfing world, a professor was just about as low as anyone could get.

I had a similar conversation at a creative writing conference at Oregon State University. During a break between scheduled events, I looked up an assistant football coach, a man who'd played quarterback there and whom I'd played against and come to know while in high school in Honolulu. After we'd reminisced a while, he suggested we go out together and have a few beers that night. "Believe me, I'd love to," I said, "but I have to go to a poetry reading."

He stared at me, wide-eyed and amazed. After a few seconds—I think it took him that long to process what I'd said—his face sagged into an expression of commiseration and gloom. "Jees," he said. "Too bad, man. I'm really sorry."

I'm not exaggerating the point. It's all too common for self-styled intellectuals to disdain athletes and everything they do, and just as common for jocks to return the favor.

Myles Brand, former president of the NCAA, and before that the University of Oregon, stated it this way: "Sports plays a central role in American culture. Yet, there is a deep reluctance—almost embarrassment—among the intellectual classes to acknowledge the enjoyment of spectator sports."

An experience I had a few Februarys ago at a Super Bowl party where most of the guests were academics corroborates Brand's conclusion. Few of those in attendance admitted to knowing, or caring about, which teams were on the field, or where the game was being played, or who was favored, or why. Eating, drinking, and bantering small talk were the order of the day, and, on the television screen, allegedly clever commercials commanded far more attention than touchdown drives. One of the few comments I heard relating to football came early in the first quarter when a gentleman sitting near me asked his wife, "How do you suppose they move that yellow line up and down the field so fast?"

Novelist Tom Wolfe expresses the countering viewpoint of athletes with this line from *I Am Charlotte Simmons*: ". . . in the mouths of coaches or recruited athletes the title Professor, all by itself, carried the connotation of 'Pretentious Fool.'"

Billy and I talked often about the problem. I told him about a boy who played tackle beside me on my college football team and who often became confused about his blocking assignment. Whenever that happened, he scratched his helmet in perplexity as we broke the huddle. I also told him about one of my English department colleagues who, while crossing the campus toward the parking lot and discussing literary criticism with a friend, walked head-on into the side of a delivery van parked outside the student union.

Eventually and thankfully, Billy decided he wanted to be a smart and responsible jock.

Now, though, the complex subject of money was proving tougher to deal with. While the brain-jock divide can be isolated and clearly defined, money profoundly affects nearly every facet of our lives: education, the environment, commerce, advertising, art, theater, entertainment, health, marriage, housing, politics—and on, and on, and on.

I was trying not to preach or to pretend I had all the answers and to resist sarcasm and oversimplification. It wasn't easy, but the fact that Billy had chosen not to be a fool gave me encouragement.

hogs, fish eyes, and ceos

. . . there warn't anybody at the church, except maybe a hog or two, for there warn't any lock on the door, and hogs like a puncheon floor in summertime because it's cool. If you notice, most folks don't go to church, only when they've got to, but a hog is different.

—Mark Twain, *The Adventures of Huckleberry Finn*

$ $ $

With the high school locked up on weekends, Billy and I met regularly at eleven o'clock at the YMCA gym for weekend shooting sessions. I sometimes arrived at the Y at ten for a workout on an elliptical machine.

A row of TV sets is mounted on a high shelf along the wall facing the exercise paraphernalia, and today I happened to be in front of a screen showing an Arnold Schwarzenegger movie. I wasn't wearing earpieces, so ignoring a steroid monster packing an oversized gun was easy enough.

After a few minutes, not quite sweating yet, I looked up and saw that Arnold had been replaced by a televangelist gesticulating in front of a stained-glass window featuring a flock of stiff-legged white sheep on a field of green. The absence of sound exaggerated the preacher's crass absurdity. Mouth moving relentlessly, stubby arms waving like an overweight bird struggling to take flight, he grimaced, laughed, and bugged his eyes out. He alternated nodding his head up and down, which condensed and expanded his multiple chins, and shaking his head back and forth, making his jowls quiver. Finally he rubbed his hands through his wavy hair, closed his eyes tightly and pointed both hands straight up, presumably toward heaven, or someone who lives there.

Then as the preacher opened his eyes and slowly lowered his arms, the camera panned to the audience, where elderly women shed visible tears and men, all of them as white as the sheep on the stained-glass window, managed to simultaneously appear both self-satisfied and ignorant.

Eight or ten seconds of audience shots were followed by a laxative commercial.

The King and Duke and their revival meeting in *Huckleberry Finn* made for hilarious fiction, but using God and religion to bilk vulnerable people in real life isn't funny. As Holden Caulfield eloquently put it, Jesus would've puked.

I remembered a middle-aged woman from one of my American literature classes. *Huckleberry Finn* had been on the reading list, and in the paper she wrote on the novel she made the confession that, as a twenty-something, she had worked as a hired performer at Billy Graham rallies. For hard cash, she had wept, wailed, and been saved in public.

When Hilde and I helped a local charity by delivering prepared meals to elderly folks and shut-ins, we encountered an old woman living alone who was being swindled by a televangelist. His program happened to be on one day when we made our delivery, and she proudly told us she never missed his show. She spoke to his onscreen image while we were there. Before we left, she assured us the preacher was her close personal friend. She had written to him the same day she saw him for the first time, had received a quick reply, and, ever since, weekly letters arrived convincing her that he knew and loved her and cared about her life. The predictable result was that she sent him a check every time he asked for money, which was every time he sent another letter.

A glance at the wall clock showed I'd been on the elliptical machine nearly fifteen minutes.

Another of my students, a young man with the biblical name of Luke, had worked nights and weekends for a southern Oregon evangelist to help pay his way through school. This preacher conducted his services in a warehouse on the outskirts of a nearby town that, after remodeling, had become a "tabernacle." After a few weeks on the job, Luke told me he hoped to get into the preaching trade himself, and the sooner the better. Two things had impressed him about the tabernacle: the services were "a crock of shit" and the preacher was "rolling in dough."

I remembered the televangelist Pat Robertson, who had solicited donations supposedly meant to aid starving African refugees. He called his nonprofit organization Operation Blessing and used the money he collected to develop his own African diamond mine. One of his pilots reported that Robertson prayed for diamonds on a flight to the Congo.

Someone had changed the TV channel. Now there were two bearded men in a drift boat on a coastal river, one with a fly rod and one at the oars.

The fishing scene brought to mind a man named Hal Riney, who, before he died, was considered one of the top advertising men in America. I knew him from the North Umpqua River, where we both fly fished for summer steelhead. Back in the early 1960s, on his own time and at his own expense, Riney produced a short, powerful film titled *Pass Creek* that exposed destructive logging practices in the Umpqua watershed and thereby helped protect the river for future generations of fish and anglers. Years later, when Ronald Reagan ran for president, Riney produced the "morning in America" ads that many believe were instrumental in getting Reagan elected. When I asked him whether he believed in Reagan or anything he stood for, Riney answered, "Hell no, but I'll do anything for enough money."

On Monday nights, Hilde and I used to watch *Fear Factor* with the grandsons, back when they were young enough to be enthralled by grossness. For a $50,000 prize, *Fear Factor* contestants competed in stunts that involved eating live insects (spiders, scorpions, cockroaches) and worms, fish eyes, bull testicles, and pizzas made with coagulated blood instead of tomato sauce. There were also physical competitions, such as having contestants dive to the bottoms of transparent tanks of water and use their mouths to retrieve the livers, brains, and hearts of various beasts. Just like Riney, these were people who'd do anything for enough money.

During the Reagan years, Hilde and I had been asked to dinner by an angling friend. Among the guests was a prominent accountant, a middle-aged man, who, like Mrs. Texas, loved to talk about money. After our meal, I found myself cornered by the accountant between a mounted steelhead and the glassy-eyed head of a well-antlered black-tail buck. Immediately the accountant regaled me with stories about some of his wealthiest clients. When he paused to sip his drink, I asked him, politely, if he could explain why people who had more money than they needed kept wanting even more and wasted their lives trying to get it.

"That's obvious," he said. "There's no *wasting* involved. Power's the only thing that really matters in life, and money's the only real power there is."

"No respected philosopher in the history of the world would agree with you on that," I answered.

He opened his eyes wide, tilted his head to the side and leaned forward, as if trying to get a close look at a peculiar form of life in an aquarium tank. "Come on," he finally said. "Philosophy? What the hell difference does philosophy make to anybody? Whoever dies with the most money wins. It's that simple."

I gave him the only possible answer. "It's even simpler. Whoever dies with the most money's dead." At that, the accountant narrowed his eyes, looked me up and down, quickly turned, and stomped away.

Hilde and I had met an old man on one of our drives down the Baja highway to Loreto on the Sea of Cortez, where we kept a fishing boat with friends. We always spent a night about halfway down the peninsula in the comfortable hotel in San Ignacio, probably Baja's nicest village. One evening after dinner, we sat on a bench underneath the big old laurel trees in the town plaza to watch children playing and town folk strolling by. An old man, clearly identifiable as an American, walked up and sat with us. After we'd exchanged small talk about the weather and the road, I asked him whether he was all alone. Without answering, head in his hands, he began weeping. When Hilde asked what was wrong, he explained he had just phoned his accountant and learned that the stock market had yielded him a profit that day of something between ten and fifteen thousand dollars. "My wife died a month ago," he said then. "We always talked about driving through Baja together. But we never did. We talked about going lots of places—Europe, Japan, China, Australia. The truth is we never did much of anything. I was always too busy working. We never had children. Of course sometimes the stocks bring less than ten thousand dollars in a day. But often it's more—substantially more. All in all, today was about average. I've made a lot of money!" With that he got up and walked back toward the hotel, frail and slow, alone in the middle of Baja.

I remembered a late afternoon spent loafing around a swimming pool at a Baja hotel after the day's fishing. Hilde and I were drinking Negra Modelo beers with chips and salsa at a table in the shade of date palms. Most Baja anglers are men, and there were a dozen or more of them at least half-drunk on margaritas at the poolside bar. They talked loudly and with great enthusiasm, all of them, about money—how much they made and how they made it, how much they spent and where they spent it, how much more they hoped for. Five young women in scant bikinis, all of them varying degrees of gorgeous, walked in single file down the steps from the hotel lobby to the swimming pool.

They passed between our table and the crowd at the bar, not ten feet away from any of us, but the men were so engrossed in their money talk that not even one of them looked at the women.

Another glance at the television screen: the drift boat anglers bounced out of a riffle and into a deep, slow pool.

$ $ $

> What I want for this country above all else is that it may always be a place where a man can get rich.
>
> —Ronald Reagan

custard pies and horsepower

I got to the gym ahead of Billy and chose a ball out of the big wire basket next to the door, dribbled it out to the free throw line, and began shooting.

An old football injury combined with age has pretty well ruined my right shoulder, but I like to think I can still hit consistently from fifteen feet. The elliptical machine had me loose, but today I missed my first four shots, three of them off the back rim. Finally I dropped one, and then five more in a row.

"Hi, Opa."

"Hey, Billy."

He'd come up behind me, and I turned and tossed him the ball.

"Keep on shooting," he said. "The stroke's going good."

"I've had plenty. I'll quit while I'm ahead."

Billy started with easy eight and ten-footers, a couple of steps between shots, making a gradual arc around the basket, then shooting twelve-footers back the other way.

"I worked out upstairs before you got here," I said. "It got me remembering things. Did your philosophy teacher ever talk much about money?"

"Not much."

"I remembered an accountant I talked to once. He didn't believe in philosophy. What he believed was that the amount of money a person had was more important than anything else. No philosophers I ever heard of thought that way."

Billy went out to three-point range and began hitting from there. I liked standing under the hoop, watching the slowly rotating orange ball arc through the air and drop, hearing it swish through the net, letting it land in my left hand, and then flipping it back out with a bounce pass.

"Seen that new *Three Stooges* movie yet?" Billy asked.

"Not yet, but I will. I grew up watching the *Stooges*. They were making movies way back in the 1930s, during the great economic depression, even before I was born. In the ones I like best they end up at rich people's dinner parties and the rich people end up with custard pies in their faces or bowls of soup dumped over their heads. The thing was, back then there were a lot of poor people and a few rich ones—sort of like it's getting to be now—and the poor ones watching the movies liked to see the stooges get some revenge."

"Wait a minute," Billy said.

I held the ball while he walked over to the chairs lined up against the wall, carried one back, and placed it about twelve feet out from the hoop, near the elbow of the free throw line. Then he trotted to the baseline, turned and sprinted out, and cut sharply around the chair. I led him with a bounce pass, and the instant he had the ball, he went high for a jump shot.

It took him seven tries to sink five jumpers, and then he went to the line for five quick free throws. "Do you think all rich people deserve pies in the face?" he asked.

He moved the chair to the other side of the free throw line.

"No. But I think the ones who get their money the wrong way do."

"What wrong way?"

"Lots of wrong ways. There's all kinds of underhanded ways—rotten ways—to make money. Swindling people. Selling people crappy, useless products or lousy ideas. Lying, bribing, cheating. Destroying the earth for a quick profit. That must be about the worst."

He missed a jumper off the front rim.

"Sometimes I wonder about the people who inherit money," I said. "There's the question as to whether or not they really deserve it."

"Do you think they do?"

"Whether they do or not, a lot of the people I've known who inherited money—I mean a lot of money—didn't end up very well off. With lots of them something seems to go wrong."

After five makes from the right side, Billy hit five more free throws, and then moved the chair farther out, to cut around it for three-point jumpers.

But after his first three-pointer, Billy stopped to tighten his laces and retie his shoes. "Remember when House lit a cigar with a fifty-dollar bill?" he said.

"Sure. He was actually making fun of the same kind of people the Three Stooges were."

"I know, that's what I meant. You and Oma should come over and watch *House* with us tomorrow night."

"Sounds good to me."

He flipped me the ball and made another cut around the chair.

Two middle school boys arrived and shot at one of the side baskets.

Soon after them came a middle-aged man with a handlebar mustache who took his time choosing a ball and then went to the hoop at the opposite end of the court and began awkwardly throwing up air balls from beyond the three-point line.

Billy began his usual finishing routine with three-pointers from straight behind the key.

"Speaking of Oma," I said, "she ran into a friend of hers from Germany at Albertson's this morning, a woman named

Christiane. Her family owns a big company over there, a bunch of factories. That's where her inherited money came from. She traveled over here on a vacation years ago, after she got divorced. She loved Ashland, bought a big house and settled down, and eventually joined Alcoholics Anonymous."

Billy missed a three-pointer. "Alcoholics Anonymous?"

"She got divorced in Germany because of her drinking. She found a German boyfriend here named Helmuth and they drank together every day, but she finally decided to quit, so she left him and joined AA. Then after 9/11 the immigration people got strict, and she wasn't a citizen, so she had to sell her house and cars and go back to Germany. Well, she's back in Ashland again on a visit, staying with Helmuth. But all he does is smoke cigarettes and drink coffee and Coke and play computer games all day, every day. He's a retired businessman who had a heart attack a while back but he won't stop smoking. Or drinking either. He asked Christiane to buy him the house he's renting but she refused. So she's going back to Germany pretty soon, but she hates it there, because she doesn't have much connection with anybody in her family, including her children. She says she can't make any friends, and she hates the weather."

Billy sank his fourth straight three-pointer, then his first jump shot.

"She has a lot more money than she needs and can't seem to find a reasonable way to live. It's not uncommon."

I knew Billy heard everything I said, and he asked occasional questions, but he seldom supported or opposed my ideas or conclusions. I didn't mind that. I'd done a lot more listening than talking to adults at that age too. When I had talked back to adults, it was often to contradict them.

I had no clear ideas about Billy's future. All I knew was what I didn't want for him. I didn't want him swayed by political bullshit, or advertising, or peer pressure, or the dozens of alluringly simple-minded clichés he heard nearly everywhere he went, every day. I didn't want him to prepare for a useless career that would earn him money but leave him hollow inside. I didn't want him turning blind to nature, or to charity, or to proper human rights, or to true friendship, or to the idea that love and family could work and endure. I didn't want the doors to his heart and soul nailed shut.

Billy had sunk four straight three-pointers, then four straight jumpers, but missed his first free throw.

"Shit," he muttered under his breath.

I bounced the ball back out and he missed a three-pointer.

"Fuck," he said.

Then he started to hit again and made his twelve shots without a miss.

The middle-aged shooter with the big mustache at the other end of the court, instead of settling for air balls, had moved in and was banging shots off the backboard and rim. When we walked by him heading toward the door, he waved and smiled.

We stowed our shoes, socks, cell phones, and car keys in an empty locker, passed by the swimming pool and turned into the hot tub room.

I submersed myself neck-deep to let a strong jet of the warm water hit my aching shoulder. Billy sat on the edge to soak his left foot, still sore two weeks after a foul tip off an inside fastball caught it squarely.

We started off talking about Billy's favorite baseball team, the Yankees, and his favorite player, Derek Jeter. So far, Jeter, who many "experts" had dismissed as old and in permanent decline, was off to an excellent start.

Then we talked about the *House* episode that featured a morbidly obese and very likable patient whose death had nothing to do with his weight, and then about the series of episodes that House spent at a treatment center resisting the care of an aggressive black psychiatrist. Billy told of an argument he'd had about *House* with a classmate who complained that all the stories were exactly the same, beginning with a complicated medical emergency that House, after false starts and difficulties, always solved at the end. To his credit, Billy had argued that the medical issues were never the real point, but were used as vehicles that allowed the various characters to interact.

Finally Billy mentioned that he'd read the article I'd left with him before baseball practice.

"What'd you think?" I asked him.

"I get the point all right."

"Muhammad Ali gave up a lot for what he believed in. He gave away the best years of his career. And it could have been even worse for him."

"Whatever happened to the two Olympic runners?"

"That was Mexico in 1968. Years later, I interviewed the American who won the high jump gold medal that year, Dick Fosbury. He told me he and nearly everybody else on the team were on Smith's and Carlos's side. He told me John Carlos had a hell of a hard time after the Olympics, but he never regretted what he did. It was the right thing. I'm not sure Tiger Woods ever did the right thing or ever even cared what it was. Instead he turned himself into a money-making machine. Then his life fell apart. Some people think he deserved it."

"What about Michael Jordan?"

"What about him? I don't know that he ever came out for or against anything—anything that matters, anything controversial—and I doubt if he ever will."

An old, bent man walked into the hot tub room on rickety legs, looked at Billy, looked at me, stepped to the edge of the tub to stick a big toe into the water, then quickly withdrew it. "That water's too fucking hot," he said and walked back out.

We sat quietly a while.

After a few minutes, perhaps influenced by the hot tub, the talk turned to water sports. I'd grown up surfing in Hawaii, and Billy and his brother Jake had tried it with some success on vacations at Waikiki and in Mexico. But wakeboarding on lakes was the popular water pastime in southern Oregon in summertime.

"You should try wakeboarding," Billy told me, not for the first time. "You could do it."

"Maybe I could," I said. "I think I could. But I guess surfing spoiled me. I'll leave it to you young guys."

"What do you have against it?"

"I don't have anything against it."

"You must have, or you'd try it at least."

"Okay, you're right. I guess I do have something against it. It's the boats and motors a lot of people use. I see hundred-horsepower outboards on huge boats at Emigrant Lake, boats you could probably make it across to Hawaii on. People who fish the lake for bluegills and crappies use fifty-horsepower, at least. The bass fishermen kick it up to seventy-five. The whole subject's a hang-up of mine. When Oma and I had our little aluminum boat in Baja, we had a fifteen-horsepower Mercury on it and that was plenty. You don't need a sledgehammer to drive in a thumbtack."

"How many times did you go to Baja?"

"Lots of times. Fifteen, twenty. I lost count. It was always fun. We always met interesting people. They usually weren't in the nicest places, the fancy restaurants and hotels we went to once in a while. We met them in the cheap hotels or at the campgrounds, the corner taco stands, all the ordinary places, places something like La Tapatia. We met young people from Europe and Japan, middle-aged women on surfing trips, graduate students doing dissertations on botany or ocean life. In the fancy places we usually met bored people complaining about the food."

$ $ $

> Most of the luxuries and many of the so-called comforts of life are not only not indispensable, but positive hindrances to the elevation of life.
>
> —Henry Thoreau

$ $ $

Driving home from the Y, two people from the distant past came unaccountably to mind.

A distant relative, Vaughn Monroe—he married my father's cousin, Marian Baughman—had been trained for opera but instead became a very popular singer in his day. "Ghost Riders in the Sky" and "Racing with the Moon" were his biggest hits. When I was about Billy's age, my father took me to visit him in his dressing room at a Las Vegas hotel before he went onstage for his show. I remember him as a kind, friendly man, not very tall, somewhat pudgy, and going bald. But the young woman who prepared him for the stage changed all that. He walked out of the dressing room wearing elevator shoes, shoulder pads worthy of a football player, what could only be described as a corset to contain his gut, and a hairpiece covering his bald spot.

An old Punahou School friend named Jim, a handsome boy, experienced some stage and screen success as a young man. But it wasn't enough success to suit him, because it didn't make him rich, so he gave up acting and made his money on the business side of movies. Eventually he earned enough to buy himself a house in Malibu. Years after the event, he told me about a trick he played at a dinner party there. The guests had been among the Hollywood elite, and during the meal, Jim raved about an extraordinary bottle of wine he was saving for them, a gift from the private cellar of a wealthy Frenchman, airmailed from Paris to Malibu for this occasion. After dessert, he carried the dark green bottle into the dining room, uncorked and wrapped in a clean white towel. Each guest was served half a crystal glassful, and every one of them marveled at the quality of the beverage. Jim had bought the wine the day before at a liquor store in downtown Los Angeles. It was rotgut, a brand preferred by the city's winos.

A few years later, Jim lost his Malibu house and not long after that, still in his fifties, he drank himself to death.

numbers in a book

Back at home I checked my emails, which consisted of pleas for money, hyperbolic alerts about political issues, the offer of a motorized wheel chair to be paid for by Medicare, an opportunity to view photos of elderly singles in my area, and a promotion for a product guaranteed to vastly enlarge my penis. (According to the subject line, after enlargement I could become the "Pied Piper of chicks." Earlier in the week, the same product had been guaranteed to transform me "from a love guru into a sex magnet . . . and also the pride of the locker room.")

There was one personal message from a friend.

Ed Jensen is a retired CEO of Visa International who graduated with me from Punahou School in 1955. Both of us high-jumped on the junior high track team, and through the years we took several classes together. Eddie, as everyone called him then, was a quiet, friendly boy, a very good if not phenomenal student, and an athlete who worked hard without a lot of success. Though we've ended up with little in common economically, socially, or politically, I like him now just as I liked him then, especially in comparison with two other wealthy Punahou graduates of our era, one said to be a Nazi sympathizer and the other a man whose wife reportedly caught him in bed with their daughter-in-law.

Like a number of Punahou alumni, the alleged Nazi and the perverse philanderer inherited valuable land, palatial homes, and vast sums of money. In contrast, Eddie is what most Americans like to admire, a self-made man. His parents weren't wealthy and I'm certain none of his business success resulted from family connections. His career started modestly at a pineapple company in Honolulu, progressed to banking and real estate on the mainland, and culminated with the Visa job.

Our email correspondence began in earnest in 2008, when I included Eddie in a Sunday feature piece I wrote for the Portland *Oregonian* about the probable influences of Punahou School and Hawaii on Barack Obama. His message today was brief and included an attachment, a *Wall Street Journal* article about another Punahou graduate and mutual friend. I read the article and soon forgot it, but there are moments I've spent with both Eddie and his wife Marilyn that I'll never forget.

Several years ago, the Jensens spent a few days at the Steamboat Inn on the North Umpqua River. I took Eddie steelhead fishing and, for a relative newcomer to the sport, he did surprisingly well on a very challenging stream. Outdoor pastimes normally make for relaxed and open conversation and, driving between the Fairview Pool and Wright Creek, I made a casual, uncalculated remark in a neutral tone of voice about the amount of money paid to CEOs.

"It's just a standard old boys network thing," Eddie said. "Everybody just has to get at least as much as the other guys in the game, or if possible more. The truth is, what CEOs get paid is obscene."

I'm certain he never said that to his peers, and I didn't press him on the issue. I accepted it as an obvious truth from a surprising source.

When Billy played for Ashland in the state Little League championship tournament in Portland, the Jensens were kind enough to invite Hilde and me to stay with them.

Their Portland house surprised me. Yes, it's a fairly large structure in a definitely upscale neighborhood, swimming pool and hot tub included, but compared to other dwellings I've visited owned by our so-called 1-percenters, its scale and furnishings are eminently modest. There were only two cars in the garage, one of them a Prius.

Another Portland surprise was a remark made by Marilyn Jensen to Hilde and me at the kitchen table one evening.

She was perplexed over the fact that Eddie had recently sold one of their homes (I believe they owned four at the time), a penthouse on Nob Hill in San Francisco. As Eddie had expressed it in *Godfather* terms, someone made him an offer he couldn't refuse. "But what difference does that make?" Marilyn said. "Our daughter lives in San Francisco. I loved our place down there. What does selling it mean? At a certain point, money becomes just numbers in a book."

While I'd been at my desk with the emails, I saw through the window when the mail truck stopped at our box. I walked out, then back to the house with a handful of junk. The only envelope that deserved attention came from the NRA. Presumably because I'd once been president of a fly-fishing and conservation club, they periodically sent me promotional material. Today's included a newsletter and, a surprise to me, a membership application. I found a felt-tipped pen, printed FUCK YOU in large letters across the application, signed my name, and sealed it into their thoughtfully provided return envelope to mail it back.

$ $ $

> Years it would take the average American household to spend a billion dollars: 20,786
>
> —Harper's Index, October 2012

the cherry wood cane

Billy's batting average, in the .500 range since his sophomore season, climbed steadily after he made his commitment to Regis. The recruiting process had been long and hard on him: daily emails, calls, and texts from coaches he'd never met at schools he'd often never heard of in places he'd never been near. Now, the decision behind him, he could finally relax.

On a chilly evening after a home game Ashland won, thanks in part to Billy's three solid base hits, I gave his father a ride home. Ron is an earnest, friendly man, an extrovert who has friends all over town. He played football and baseball for Ashland High in the early 1980s and, as an adult, donates a lot of his free time to coaching youth sports. He's as good with boys as anyone I've ever seen.

I backed out of my parking space.

"Can I talk to you about a problem?" he said.

"Sure," I answered. "What kind of problem?"

"It's about Billy. You two are close. I know I can confide in you about it."

"Sure," I said again.

"He's talking a lot these days about getting rich. It's seems like it's going too far. He says he wants to live in a mansion, drive a Hummer. If he can't make big money as a player, he thinks he might want to be an agent, like Dave Stewart down in San Diego."

I headed up the hill toward town.

I'd met Stewart, a pitcher nicknamed Smoke, a World Series MVP for Oakland in 1986, a friend of Ron's who had watched Billy play two years earlier, declaring him "a man among boys."

It took me a while to answer. "He's really talking like that?" I finally said.

"He is."

"I guess I'm surprised," I said. "But he's young. I can still remember what that's like, so you must too. I'll talk to him though. I've been talking to him all along and I'll keep it up."

I did indeed remember what it was like to be young, when I tended to believe what my best friends told me and often said what I thought they wanted to hear. At Billy's age, I'd dreamed of owning a flashy sports car, either an MG or an Austin Healy. But hearing that Billy wanted to drive a Hummer disappointed me anyway.

I also remembered my grandfather, who I'd known as a boy back in western Pennsylvania, a man who'd been locally famous for hating motor vehicles. As a young man in the early 1900s, he walked through the town of Jeanette carrying a heavy cherry wood cane he surely didn't need, and which he used to pummel any moving car that came within striking distance. He'd shattered windshields and dented hoods and fenders all over town.

And now, when I knew a retired CEO who drove a Prius, my grandson wanted a Hummer. Over four generations, things change.

saws, wheelbarrows, woodpiles

The next morning, our son, Pete, came out to our place with his chainsaw to bring down a large, dying Douglas fir, a job that gave me just the therapy I needed.

He felled the fir between some oaks and a pear tree, then sawed off the limbs, and finally worked his way down the long trunk cutting it into short logs. Meanwhile, I dragged the limbs to the burn pile and then used a handsaw to cut them into manageable lengths. After that, Pete and I loaded the logs two at a time into the wheelbarrow and took turns pushing them uphill and around the house to dump them into a pile near our storage shed.

Thoughts came and went. The day was clear and warm and soon I was sweating hard.

Small flocks of Canada geese in loose Vs flew overhead as we worked, and nesting scrub jays scolded from the oak trees.

When all the logs had been moved, we cleaned up the remaining debris where the fir had come down and took it to the burn pile. Then we lined up the logs against the shed wall to keep them out of the rain.

After Pete left, I decided to take advantage of the pleasant weather. I got the axe from the shed and began splitting wood. I enjoyed hoisting the heavy logs one after another up onto the chopping block, and I liked handling the axe, getting all my weight behind it, striking the logs dead-center, splitting them down the middle, then splitting the halves, and finally the quarters.

After I stacked the split wood, I called it a day.

$ $ $

> So many new thoughts come into your head when your hands are busy with hard physical work, when your mind has set you a task that can be achieved by physical effort and that brings its reward in joy and success, when for six hours on end you dig or hammer, scorched by the life-giving breath of the sky. And it isn't a loss but a gain that these transient thoughts, intuitions, analogies are not put down on paper but forgotten. The

town recluse whipping up his nerves and his imagination with strong black coffee and tobacco doesn't know the strongest drug of all—good health and real necessity.

—Boris Pasternak, *Doctor Zhivago*

2

cool head main t'ing

Wealthy people are the glittering scum that floats upon the deep river of production.

—Winston Churchill

curly and ripper

Late on an overcast morning, I drove about fifteen miles north from Ashland on Interstate 5, then headed eastward over a pot-holed two-lane county road. I had an appointment to interview an ex-convict named Kirk who lived in a rural area I'd never visited before. We'd made arrangements by phone, and he'd given me what seemed like clear directions, but I got lost twice. Finally I found the place, an old white trailer in a weed field off an unpaved road.

The interview was on behalf of a lawyer named Ralph Temple who had moved to southern Oregon from Washington, DC, and whose long career there had mostly involved civil rights issues, including work in the Sixties with Martin Luther King. Though nominally retired, now he was putting together a report examining the allegedly brutal treatment of prisoners at Medford's Jackson County Jail.

I parked alongside the gravel driveway leading to the trailer, climbed out of my Subaru, took two or three steps, and watched two snarling pit bulls squirm out from underneath the trailer and charge straight across the yard at me. With no time to make it back to the car, I stood my ground.

The dogs—one a mottled brown, the other black—stopped no more than a yard away and crouched there, growling and snarling.

"Keep it up and I'll kick you sons of bitches into orbit," I said, just so they could hear my voice.

They kept it up, but came no closer.

"Anybody home?" I yelled at the trailer.

A young woman wearing jeans and a gray sweatshirt appeared on the rickety porch. "Curly! Ripper! Get your asses over here!"

The dogs turned at once and trotted back to the trailer.

"Sorry about the mutts," the young woman said. "Who're you?"

"I'm supposed to meet Kirk. He said he'd be here."

Side by side, the dogs walked up the steps to the porch. The young woman eyed me warily. She had brown skin, dark eyes, and long black hair tied into a single braid that hung down her back. I judged her to be American Indian.

"What's it about?" she said. "You some kind of bill collector?"

"Me? No. I'm helping a guy who's writing a report about the lousy treatment of prisoners at Jackson County Jail. Kirk said he'd talk to me about it."

That triggered a quick transformation. She invited me onto the porch, we shook hands, and she introduced herself—her name was Nina—and explained that her husband had been summoned into town unexpectedly to help a friend who'd been in a car wreck. While we talked, I stooped to scratch Curly and Ripper between the ears.

Nina reached Kirk on a cell phone and made arrangements for me to meet him at a diner a few miles back toward town. While she talked, a boy of five or six peeked through the screen door behind her, then quickly disappeared.

After Nina gave me directions to the diner, we talked for a while. She mentioned that Kirk had been an outstanding high school basketball player with hopes to play in college until his arrest for marijuana possession landed him in jail. So that I could spot him, I asked her what he looked like, and for the first time since I'd been there, she smiled. "He looks like a young version of you," she said.

Despite the fact that her directions had seemed clear enough, I got lost yet again, so the drive took five or ten minutes more than it should have.

The diner was a wooden building painted green. The parking lot out front was crowded. I found a space next to an old Chevy pickup loaded with firewood and then walked inside, where it was warm and crowded, mostly with the same kinds of working men who eat tacos at La Tapatia.

I had no idea what to expect. Over a period of months, I'd interviewed several ex-convicts for Ralph Temple, and some had been about as friendly as Curly and Ripper coming out from under the trailer.

A quick scan of the room showed only one young man who fit Nina's description, sitting at a table for two against a window near the door. When I looked at him, he smiled and waved.

The interview was easy. We drank coffee while we talked, and the whole time, despite the subject matter, Kirk kept a surprisingly cheerful smile on his face. Yes, he and two friends had been arrested with marijuana in the car. It was his third drug arrest, so he did time at the county jail. Then, on probation, he had missed an appointment with his parole officer. He had called the office a day early to say he couldn't be there, and to explain why, but there was no record of the call, and he was arrested again and jailed for parole violation. The arrest itself was the major issue.

He described it this way: "Four deputies came out to the trailer. All I was doing was handing one of them my ID. I wasn't doing anything else. I didn't provoke anybody. I didn't say a word. I handed over my ID and then all of a sudden the deputies jumped me and pinned me down and beat me in front of my whole family. My five-year-old son and my eighty-year-old grandmother were watching."

Afterward, at the jail, despite his requests, he had been refused medical treatment.

I wondered what could be affecting Kirk now, why he was smiling. As if reading my mind, he explained:

"The good news is, I got a job! Just yesterday it happened. A tree company hired me. Arborists is what they call those tree people. All I'll do at first is cleanup work, under the trees and all, loading limbs and branches into the chipper, but the boss says he'll teach me to climb and handle a chain-saw if everything works out. It'll work out! I guarantee it will! I start tomorrow! It's the best damn thing that's happened to me in two years!"

"Congratulations," I said, and I reached across the table to shake his hand.

"Thanks, man!"

"It's a real coincidence. My son's an arborist."

"Well now I'm one too!"

A joyful smile lit up Kirk's clean-shaven face and, looking across the table at me, a light shined from his clear brown eyes.

My last order of business was to ask whether he'd sign his name to a copy of the interview if I mailed it to him.

"Hell yes!" he said. "No problem! I'll never go back to that jail again, I'll guarangoddamntee you that! I got me a job!"

I'm not sure I've ever met a stranger to whom I took such an immediate liking.

$ $ $

Back on I-5 with the traffic light and the car on cruise control, thoughts about Kirk and his arrest led to reflections about marijuana.

In 1985, my son and I drove to northern California's Humboldt County for the Avenue of the Giants Marathon. The run through the ancient trees went well for both of us, and the trip gave me a close, quick look at the area's pot-growing subculture.

After the run, on the way back to our hotel, I stopped at a rural market for two cans of root beer and ended up in the checkout line behind three bearded, long-haired men, each of whom, when paying for his groceries, produced a leather wallet stuffed with bills—mostly twenties, from what I could see.

By the time I'd paid with my five-dollar-bill, the front door had closed behind the three affluent customers. The cashier, a young woman, saw me looking after them and must have read the surprised look on my face, because she shook her head with a furtive smile and then nodded in their direction. "Growers," she said as she handed over my change. "Fact is, they keep this place going. Fact is, they keep everything going around here. They're pretty good citizens no matter what anybody says."

Northern California began welcoming the so-called counterculture in the late '60s, when the hippies headquartered in San Francisco spread out. On remote hillsides and in quiet valleys, "mom and pop" marijuana operations discreetly flourished. Married or unmarried couples, or a few close friends, worked to grow and sell enough pot to own a small home, pay the bills, and maybe take a vacation to Mexico in the wintertime. Hardly anybody in the area seemed disturbed about it. In fact, local radio stations went so far as to announce the whereabouts of state troopers as a public service.

But in recent years, taking advantage of liberalized marijuana laws, ambitious large-scale commercial producers have moved in aggressively. These new entrepreneurs represent big money, or what the accountant I'd talked to at the dinner party defined as "power." They clear-cut hillsides to create growing space, use dangerous pesticides, and drain pristine creeks into their irrigation canals. Some of them cultivate indoors, with generators to power the growing lights in greenhouses that cover an acre or more. Instead of driving Toyotas, the newcomers roam the countryside in luxury cars and SUVs. Among pot-growers, as well as ranchers and farmers, the old ways of life are all but gone.

$ $ $

I turned the radio on to catch the hourly news and was immediately informed of a more absurd and extravagant manifestation of greed than anything related to marijuana. In the customary neutral and resonant voice, a newscaster told of a man named John Thain, former CEO of Merrill Lynch, a Wall Street firm that failed spectacularly during America's financial meltdown. Even as the collapse developed and progressed, Thain had his office remodeled at a cost exceeding a million dollars. The renovations included a $35,000 toilet.

That was more than enough news. I turned the radio off and wondered what variety of warped human being could spend that sum of money, his or anybody else's, on a toilet. No matter how twisted he might be, must be, I found it hard to believe that Thain, or anybody else, could think that highly of his ass or his shit. The exorbitant toilet had to be meant to serve as a topic of conversation, something to casually mention while waiting to tee off at a restricted country club, or sipping scotch on the deck of a yacht.

The yacht deck thought took me to the memory of another former student. A woman I knew spent her winters in Florida and sold yachts there, not sailboats, no mere ketches or schooners, but the huge engine-powered boats purchased by the wealthiest among us. At a dinner party, she suggested that if I had any kids in my classes who wanted to travel and would like well-paid summer work, I could have them contact her about crewing on big boats anchored in Florida.

A student I knew well, a football player from Hawaii who had grown up working on boats, contacted the yacht woman and took a summer job as a crewman. When I ran into him on campus soon after he returned to college for the fall semester, I asked him how it had gone. He smiled shamefacedly, shook his head, and looked at the ground when he answered. "Well," he said, "it was interesting. I mean *weird*. There wasn't that much to it. There wasn't *anything* to it as far as sailing was concerned. The boat I crewed on hardly ever left the dock. The owner had parties onboard, always on weekdays. His friends would be there, other old dudes, and all kinds of young women. *Gorgeous* young women. I'm not sure they were whores. I'm pretty sure some of them were. *Most* of them in fact. *All* of them maybe. The main thing they told us in training for the job was to be damn sure we never mentioned the parties or those women to the wives and families that came onboard on the weekends. It totally weirded me out. But I kept my mouth shut on the weekends. I made damn good money too."

$ $ $

Back at home, Hilde was on the kitchen phone with her sister Elizabeth in Germany.

In 1970, near the beginning of West Germany's *Wirtschafts-wunder* (economic miracle), Elizabeth had married an ambitious young man named Otto. Whenever we visited Germany, his friendship was a pleasure. He was smart, funny, gracious, generous, and, as Bavarians are known for, loved to have a good time. I liked Otto so much that I named my first bird dog, a German shorthair, after him.

For many years, Otto the man gained economic ground along with his country. He worked his way steadily up in a firm that manufactured and sold industrial machinery, a business that did extremely well all along and then did better than ever after East and West Germany reunited.

When Hilde and I visited in 1990, Otto and Elizabeth, who had both grown up in working-class families, lived in an impressive penthouse in Furth, a town adjacent to Nurnberg. Otto drove a big new Mercedes, Elizabeth drove a big new BMW, while their son Harold had to settle for a not-quite-so-big BMW.

Then, a couple of years later during their phone conversations, Elizabeth began telling Hilde about troubling changes. Otto was drinking more than ever, and schnapps instead of beer, and he chain-smoked, slept too much, and often seemed irritable and depressed.

With each succeeding phone call, the bad news worsened.

After months of this disturbing behavior, Otto, on a winter night, drove his Mercedes to a wooded area outside Nurnberg, parked in a lonely spot, put the barrel of a pistol into his mouth, and pulled the trigger.

For years he had been embezzling large sums from his company and had finally been discovered. Though no one in the family knew a thing about it, he had already been assigned a date to appear in court on formal charges. The good money he'd made just hadn't been enough.

foul balls

On a warm and pleasant day, Hilde and I drove to North Mountain Park to watch Ashland play a doubleheader against Klamath Falls. At this point in the season, both Billy and his team were doing very well, already looking ahead toward the state playoffs.

A reassuring sense of serenity affected me whenever I saw the clean uniforms, the green outfield, the groomed infield, the precisely marked baselines and batter's box, the white bases themselves, the distant fences behind it all, and the scoreboard just beyond the left field fence. At a baseball game, I could always forget toilet seats and yacht parties, even suicides, for a few languid hours.

Billy was a right-handed batting first baseman, and Hilde and I sat between home plate and first base. We always arrived about half an hour early to claim our accustomed seats and to watch the pitchers warm up and the infielders take ground balls.

There was little drama in game one. Billy went three-for-five, including two doubles, and from the third inning on, there was no doubt about the outcome.

In the eighth inning, one of Billy's teammates fouled a pitch high over the backstop straight behind home plate, and from where we were sitting, I could watch the ball's trajectory all the way, rising small and white against a clean blue sky, seeming to stop momentarily at the apex, then dropping straight down and—I saw it coming before it happened—crashing loudly through the sunroof of a shiny green Mercedes sedan.

Conspicuous signs warn drivers who park behind the backstop that they do so at their own risk, so it's logical to argue that anybody ignoring the signs deserves whatever he gets. Whether the Mercedes owner had it coming or not, the foul ball led to a conversation I was glad to have with Billy. I'd been reminding myself, often, to be careful not to force any issue with him, to do my best not to lecture. But I took advantage of my chances when they came, and the shattered sunroof soon produced an opening.

Hilde always brought food and a Gatorade for Billy to have between games of a doubleheader, and after the team's post-game rituals—high-fiving and fist-bumping opposing team members, then meeting for a few minutes in a large huddle in shallow left field with the coaches—he hurried across the infield and around the backstop, metal cleats loud on the concrete walkway. He came up to us smiling, the left leg of his uniform smeared with dirt from sliding into second base, the chest smeared from diving headfirst back into the same base on a pick-off attempt.

Sitting between us, he ate his sandwich first, then the apple, then the homemade cookies, and finally washed it down with the Gatorade while the three of us talked about the way the game had gone.

It was after Hilde left to visit Ingrid, who was working the concession stand, that the smashed sunroof came up.

"Do you know whose car that foul ball hit?" Billy asked me.

"No idea. Nobody's been over there inspecting the damage yet."

"It must be somebody at the game."

"Maybe they don't know it happened."

"I couldn't see it from the dugout but I heard it. It was a pretty loud crash."

"Yes it was."

We were looking at the Mercedes when two eight or nine-year-old boys walked up and stood beside the car, staring at it, talking and pointing, finally shading their eyes with their hands to see inside, where the seats must have been littered with fragments of glass.

"It's probably just as well that an expensive one got it," I said, "because whoever it belongs to must have good insurance."

"What kind is it?"

"A Mercedes, a German car. We see them pretty much all over the place when we visit Oma's hometown. But they're more common there than they are here. What kind of cars do you like?"

"SUVs are cool. What about you?"

"We're happy with our Subaru," I said. "Good gas mileage. So far, only one small repair bill in over ninety thousand miles."

"Hummers are cool."

"How come you think so?"

"Mostly I guess because not that many people have one."

"Maybe so," I said, "but it's hard to see why that makes much difference. A lot of the things we own perform pretty simple functions. A watch tells time. See this?" I held out my left wrist. "That's the cheapest Swiss Army watch made, I got it for I think about fifty bucks in Germany, and it's been keeping perfect time for years. A Rolex must cost at least twenty times as much but it's no better than this. It couldn't be. All it does is tell time."

"I don't even have a watch," Billy said. "My cell phone tells the time."

"Does an expensive cell phone tell time any better than a cheap one?"

"It does other things better."

"Our Subaru gets us where we want to go as well as any Mercedes would. As well or better."

"Maybe it's not as comfortable though."

"All modern cars are comfortable enough."

"Maybe it's not as safe."

"The way you drive a car has a lot more to do with how safe it is than anything else. Brand names, expensive stuff, is mostly for snob appeal. Oma carries a purse. Maybe it cost twenty or thirty bucks. Or less. She could buy a purse for thousands of dollars—I'm not kidding, people buy expensive crap like that—and she'd still be carrying the same stuff in it."

"Look," Billy said. "Those must be the owners."

A tall, red-faced, bowlegged man in khaki shorts and a Seattle Seahawks sweatshirt with a tiny woman beside him, probably his wife, also wearing khaki shorts, but with a long-sleeved white blouse, stood beside the Mercedes now, obviously arguing. The man, hands on his hips, was bent at the waist, talking nonstop at the woman, who, standing on tiptoes, was talking back nonstop and wagging an index finger at him, almost touching his red nose.

"One of them must have wanted to park there and the other one didn't and that happened," Billy said.

We watched the argument.

They went at it hard, heads wagging, arms gesticulating, for at least two minutes. Finally the man peeled off his Seahawks sweatshirt—he wore a baggy white T-shirt underneath—and opened the driver's side door. With his hand wrapped in the sweatshirt, he scraped glass off the front seat out onto the parking lot. Then the two of them climbed in, backed up, and sped off, the man driving, the woman staring balefully up through the sunroof.

"Do you know much about the NRA?" Billy asked me after they were out of sight.

This was a lucky day—another opening. "Sure," I said. "Some. Why?"

"We're talking about it in social studies and I might have to write a paper on it. What do you think about them?"

"The NRA? I think they suck."

"Any ideas for a paper?"

"Humor can work, even with a serious subject. You could start off in your title by giving them a new name—Nitwits, Reactionaries, and Assholes. Or I guess the N could stand for Numbskulls. Or Neanderthals."

"How come you think they suck?"

"More reasons than I can remember all at once. The main one is that their leaders and lawyers make money from gun manufacturers and for gun manufacturers, a hell of a lot of money. They do everything they can to make sure the manufacturers can sell guns to people who shouldn't have them."

"Don't they defend the constitution?"

"That's what they claim. But the constitution, it's the second amendment, can be interpreted in different ways. Read it and see what you think. Or the constitution might be just plain wrong. It was written by people. People make mistakes. And the people who wrote it said so themselves. Times change. They knew times would change. We've gone from muskets to assault weapons. Don't take my word for anything. Find out all you can, think about it, and make up your own mind. Just make sure you think."

"What about their motto—'Guns don't kill people, people do'?"

"That's bumper sticker bullshit. Look up the figures. We have about 5 percent of the world's population and at least 50 percent of the world's guns. We have about thirty thousand gun deaths including at least ten thousand murders a year. Germany might have a hundred murders a year. It's easy to look stuff up online these days. Just make sure of your source."

"I will."

"Once you do, then make up your mind."

"I'll do it."

"And don't use that 'asshole' title unless you're sure your teacher won't mind."

Another luxury vehicle pulled into the parking space vacated by the Mercedes, this one a Lincoln Navigator.

"No sunroof on that one," I said to Billy, "but I guess you guys can try for the front windshield."

A well-dressed middle-aged couple climbed out of the Navigator, and these two also appeared to be arguing, both talking at once, the woman nodding her head and the man shaking his. Instead of coming toward the ball field, they turned abruptly away from one another and, walking fast, headed off in opposite directions, the woman down Mountain Avenue toward Ashland Creek, the man uphill toward town.

Ashland won a close Game Two, with Billy going two-for-four, and no foul balls cleared the backstop.

On the drive home, I slowed so we could watch two big brown steers fighting over a pile of alfalfa hay in a pasture. Just as one of them tried to bite into the hay, the other one forced it away with his shoulder, something like an offensive lineman throwing a block. When the steer that threw the block turned back to the hay, his rival charged hard and knocked him sideways with a head-butt. A few yards away from the hay they were fighting for lay an identical pile of hay they both ignored. It's a sad thing to see innocent animals acting like people.

$ $ $

At the gunshop nothing was furtive, nobody was embarrassed, and the clientele, so far as Delaney could see, consisted of average ordinary citizens in shorts and college sweatshirts, business suits and dresses, shopping for the tools of murder as casually as they might have shopped for rat traps or gopher pellets at the hardware store.

—T. C. Boyle, *The Tortilla Curtain*

assholes

As geese honked from our neighbor's pond and four sleek does grazed an adjoining hillside, I sat under an oak tree and read a *New York* Magazine article authored by Lisa Miller. The piece reached some provocative conclusions about the rich.

Miller began by relating disturbing facts: ". . . the top fifth of American families have seen their incomes rise by 45 percent since 1979, whereas the bottom fifth has seen a decline of 11 percent . . . The top 20 percent of Americans own about 87 percent of the wealth; the bottom 80 percent splits the rest. Social mobility, never as attainable as imagined, is stagnant. Forty percent of Americans inhabit the same social class as their grandparents, making the United States less socially mobile than Japan or France."

She went on to quote an article titled "Higher Social Class Predicts Increased Unethical Behavior," written by Paul Piff and published in *Proceedings of the National Academy of Sciences*: ". . . living high on the socioeconomic ladder can, colloquially speaking, dehumanize people. It can make them less ethical, more selfish, more insular, and less compassionate than other people . . . While money doesn't necessarily make anybody anything, the rich are way more likely to prioritize their own self-interests above the interests of other people. It makes them more likely to exhibit characteristics that we would stereotypically associate with, say, assholes."

Miller summarized what she called "Piff's most notorious research," consisting of observations that did indeed portray rich folks as assholes: "Last year, he (Piff) spent three months hanging out at the intersection of Interstate 80 and Lincoln Highway, near the Berkeley Marina . . . Piff and his research team would stake out the intersection at rush hour, crouching behind a bank of shrubs near the Sea Breeze Market and Deli, and catalogue cars that came by, giving each vehicle a grade from one to five (five would be a new-model Mercedes, say, and one would be an old, battered Honda like the one Piff drives). Then the researchers would observe the drivers' behavior. A third of the people who drove grade-five cars, Piff found, rolled into the intersection without first coming to a complete stop—a violation, he reminds readers in his PNAS study, of the California

Vehicle Code . . . When Piff designed a similar experiment to test drivers' regard for pedestrians, in which a researcher would enter a zebra crossing as a car approached it, the results were more staggering . . . fully half the grade-five cars cruised right into the crosswalk."

My grandfather, who enjoyed smashing hoods, fenders, and windshields with his cherry wood cane, would have appreciated Piff's research, and I wish he could have been there to do his best work when grade-five cars violated the crosswalk.

When I finished the article, I carried the magazine across the yard to the garage and tossed it into the car to give to Billy as suggested reading.

$ $ $

Back under the oak tree, I saw that the does had grazed farther down the hillside, closer to the pond. There were no ducks or geese in the clear sky, but scrub jays scolded loudly from a nearby incense cedar.

Over the years, I've developed a relationship with the neighborhood jays. Each morning after breakfast, while Hilde and I sit at the table talking and sipping coffee, I scatter a large handful of bread or cracker crumbs on the railing outside the big glass door separating the deck from the dining room. Then I ring the dinner bell that sits on the railing, and the jays, trained like Pavlov's dogs, soar in from the surrounding trees for their handout. A couple of them have become bold enough to eat from the palm of my hand.

If I'm more than a few minutes late with the crumbs, a jay or two will often sit on the arm of the deckchair nearest the window, staring in at us, squawking loudly. If I'm doing yard work or splitting wood later in the day, the birds scold from nearby branches, hoping for an extra snack, which they get only occasionally. I don't want to encourage dependency and turn them into welfare bums.

They scolded loudly at me today, and I ignored them. All I wanted to do was relax, remember, and reflect.

I had little doubt about many rich people being assholes, certainly some of the time, often much of the time, possibly most of the time in extreme cases. But accepting Lisa Miller's premise created as many questions as answers. Exactly what accounts for rich people who aren't assholes? Certainly there are rich people—we could all make our own lists—who seem kind, humble, charitable, humane. A few are even—that appalling adjective/noun loathed by all right-wingers—*liberal*. Obviously there are poor and middle-income assholes, and if one of them somehow becomes rich, does it make him an even bigger asshole? Or, looking at it in reverse, if a rich asshole loses his fortune and becomes middle-class or poor, does he become a better person, or could it make him a bigger asshole than ever, but for different reasons? Are people who inherit money doomed at birth to be assholes, no matter what?

With that thought, I recalled some born-rich people I'd observed in Idaho years ago when I visited Ketchum to write an article on Ernest Hemingway, who killed himself and is buried there. Olympic gold medallist Dick Fosbury lived and worked as an engineer in town and showed me around the Ketchum-Sun Valley area. The Month was October, the fall colors gorgeous, the weather ideal. Though it was during working hours on a weekday, almost everywhere we went, there were crowds of young men and women in their twenties and thirties driving the streets in expensive cars, strolling along the sidewalks, walking in and out of shops, crowding bars and cafes, eating and drinking.

"Who *are* all these people?" I finally asked my host.

Fosbury shrugged and answered matter of factly, "Every year they show up early for the ski season. Bored I guess. Killing time. They're just trust-fund trash."

I wonder what percentage of them were assholes.

$ $ $

> We are not the kind of people that would ever want to leave any of our children a trust fund. We have given you decent educations, and you are fine on your own.

> We want the pleasure of watching our grandchildren go to great schools and summer camps and take trips and have adventures. That is the pleasure money can bring—not stockpiling it so some spoiled offspring can have it when he or she turns 21.
>
> —Rear Admiral Chester Nimitz Jr., *Slate Magazine*

$ $ $

Yes, I regard money as a necessary evil. My recurrent question is, how much of the evil does a person actually need, and how low should a person stoop to get it if he really needs it? And where does intelligence fit into the equation? I've spent much of my adult life around professors, who are presumed to be intelligent, or at the least formally educated, and few of them are rich, but a fair number of them are assholes.

Many years ago, the issue of merit pay came up at Southern Oregon University. Administrators, under pressure from the State Board of Higher Education, ordered each academic department to meet and formulate procedures that would identify superior teachers, who would then be rewarded with merit-pay raises.

There were twenty-two members in our English department, and we met several times to discuss and debate the matter. Opinions varied somewhat, but all twenty-two of us agreed on one thing: there was no legitimate way to accurately define good teaching, much less identify it.

Perhaps the strongest case to be made against a merit-pay system was offered by a colleague who described a study done at an Ivy League university where undergraduates evaluated their teachers and identified those they believed to be outstanding. Then, five years after graduation, the same former students assessed the same teachers and came to radically different conclusions about them. Clearly, their experiences out in the "real world" had changed their minds about which teachers had actually done them the most good.

I argued that a merit-pay system based on student evaluations would lead to faculty members competing in shameful popularity contests. The professors who told the funniest jokes, who were the best entertainers, and who gave the highest grades would undoubtedly get the pay raises. I probably exaggerated when I offered the possibility that we might end up with the most covetous teachers serving pizza and beer in their classes, but I don't think I overstated the case by much.

The ultimate result of our many meetings was a letter to the dean of arts and sciences explaining why the English Department stood against implementing any system leading to merit-pay raises.

Predictably enough, our letter was ignored. The administration introduced a merit-pay system based on student evaluations, whether we wanted it or not. But they did offer a choice. Teachers who wanted to be considered for merit pay had to sign up for it, while those opposed to the system could refuse to sign and thereby opt out.

All but two of us signed up for merit-pay consideration, and the two of us who didn't sign were generally thought to be fools by the twenty who did.

$ $ $

My thoughts backtracked to Hemingway, to an assessment he had made of professors, labeling them "the lice that feed on literature."

Hemingway was a writer whose early work—*In Our Time* and *The Sun Also Rises*—was widely and justly admired. The piece I wrote about him after my Idaho trip examined his decline as both a writer and a man. The First World War novel *A Farewell to Arms* earned worldwide acclaim, but *Across the River and Into the Trees*, on the next war, was regarded by most of its readers as an embarrassment.

The degree to which Hemingway's life had deteriorated by the time *Across the River* came out in 1950 is made clear by his comments about James Jones in a letter he wrote to his publisher, Charles Scribner, in 1951. Jones's book *From Here to Eternity*, published that year by Scribner, earned wide and well-deserved praise, and apparently Hemingway couldn't stand it. His rant to Scribner includes this: "About the James (Jones) book: It is not great no matter what they tell you . . . He has a genius for respecting the terms of a kitchen and he is a K. P. boy for keeps and for always. Things will catch up with him and he will probably commit suicide . . . Probably I should re-read it again to give you a truer answer. But I do not have to eat an entire bowl of scabs to know they are scabs; nor suck a boil to know it is a boil; nor swim through a river of snot to know it is snot. I hope he kills himself as soon as it does not damage his or your sales. If you give him a literary tea you might ask him to drain a bucket of snot and then suck the puss out of a dead nigger's ear . . . I am glad he makes you money and I would never laugh him off. I would just give him a bigger bucket on the snot detail. He has the psycho's urge to kill himself and he will do it."

By all accounts, Hemingway had been a happy Michigan youngster who loved fishing and hunting, then an honorable soldier in Italy, and, after his war, a good husband and disciplined young writer in 1920s Paris. He worked hard in obscurity to develop a muscular, understated style that would transform twentieth-century American literature.

Everything bad that happened to him appears to have resulted from success and the money that accompanied it. He divorced his wife Hadley. Through middle-age and beyond, he was an incorrigible drunk surrounded by sycophants, a blustering macho oaf, a crude and vulgar jerk to the three wives that followed Hadley.

A friend of mine, a journalist named Harvey Meyerson, knew Hemingway and associated with him periodically through the last decade of the author's life. More than once, Harvey tried to talk to the man, reason with him, somehow help him, and, unsurprisingly, got nothing but verbal abuse for his efforts. Then, at age sixty-one, the once great writer, ten years after he had vindictively predicted James Jones's suicide, put the barrels of his favorite shotgun into his mouth and blew his own head off.

A Moveable Feast, a memoir of the early Paris years, was published posthumously. Somehow in that book, Hemingway captured some of the magic of his early work. And here is his closing line:

But this is how Paris was in the early days when we were very poor and very happy.

$ $ $

Back braced comfortably against the oak tree, I gazed out at the Siskiyou and Cascade mountains, range after range stretching into hazy distance. Looking at mountains brought to mind a thirty-four-year-old Ashland ultra-distance runner named Hal Koerner, winner of the 2012 Hardrock

100-miler in Colorado, said to be the toughest endurance run on planet Earth. Koerner, who owns a running shoe and apparel store in town, completed the punishing event in 24 hours and 50 minutes. This included 68,000 feet of climbing and descending, with the low elevation point at 7,680 feet, the high point at 14,098, and an average elevation of 11,186—quite an impressive day of work.

When I ran into Hal at the Y, back in town and working out just days after his win, I was surprised to see him looking fresh and energetic.

"The course was pretty tough," he told me matter-of-factly. "One seven-thousand-foot-climb after another. You get up over a mountain and down the other side, and there's another mountain, another seven-thousand-foot climb. Over and over and over again. But I feel fine now."

Having completed a number of marathons and a few fifty-milers, I know something about long runs, but I can't imagine struggling through rugged terrain at high elevation all day and all night for one hundred miles.

Koerner belongs to a tiny band of athletes who do such things, men and women with every right to be proud of their extraordinary physical accomplishments. As a rule, though, ultra-runners are unassuming types who rarely draw attention to themselves.

Sitting under the oak tree, I found myself contrasting Hal Koerner with my favorite asshole, Donald Trump. I regard

Koerner as representing men and women who work hard and never boast about their rare achievements, and Trump as his polar opposite: a pretentious blowhard, a physical nonentity, a tiresome joke.

$ $ $

> Beside them, little pot-bellied men in light suits and panama hats; clean, pink men with puzzled, worried eyes. Worried because formulas do not work out, hoping for security and yet sensing its disappearance from the earth. In their lapels the insignia of lodges and service clubs, places where they can go and, by a weight of numbers of little worried men, reassure themselves that business is noble and not the curious ritualized thievery they know it is; that businessmen are intelligent in spite of the records of their stupidity; that they are kind and charitable in spite of the principles of sound business; that their lives are rich instead of the thin tiresome routines they know; and that a time is coming when they will not be afraid anymore.
>
> —John Steinbeck, *The Grapes of Wrath*

$ $ $

Four turkey vultures circled lazily, high in the clear sky. In flight and seen from a distance, they might be the loveliest birds on Earth, but up close on the ground, possibly the ugliest. These four had discovered a warm air current directly over the lonely draws where I'd once hunted mountain quail with two brothers from Texas who taught me all I needed to know about the ways rich men can squander money.

Through the lives of three wonderful bird dogs, I was a near fanatical mountain quail hunter, often hiking and climbing fifteen or twenty miles through remote country in a morning or afternoon. I've never kept written records of hunting or fishing, but, despite the fact that I shot well enough, I'd guess that I averaged no more than one bird killed for every five miles I covered.

Mountain quail are wild birds, fast runners, and strong fliers, usually found in heavy cover, and for these reasons hardly anybody hunts them. I had my favorite places to myself, and after my first few years, I knew I'd increased quail populations there. There were two large coveys when I began, and by breaking up a covey and chasing a few birds a mile or more into a new creek bed or willow draw, another large covey occasionally formed and grew to populate the new area. By the time I gave the sport up—too many new landowners posting "no trespassing" signs and blocking access to public land—there were five big coveys where, in the beginning, there had been just the two. That healthy population of birds was one reason I didn't mind taking the Texans there. The other reason was my curiosity about the kind of men they'd be.

I'd published an article about mountain quail in *National Wildlife* magazine, the brothers had read it, and one of them called me up. He introduced himself as Ben, and he wondered if I might consider taking him and his brother Robert hunting to the places I'd described. He explained that they were determined to achieve a "grand slam" of American quails—bobwhites, Gambel's, scaled, California, and mountain. The first four species were already mounted and displayed in their trophy rooms, but mountain quail were proving difficult. Ben and Robert had already spent a week in Idaho with an expensive guide, where they hadn't so much as seen a bird, and they were growing desperate.

I could tell Ben was surprised when I said I'd take them hunting, and even more surprised when I said I didn't want to be paid for it. When I explained that the hunting would be physically demanding, he assured me they'd be fit and ready.

The brothers arrived at the Medford airport on a blustery Friday night in December.

With my golden retriever Luke, I took them hunting on a showery Saturday morning. They were obviously wealthy men, and they made sure I knew it by telling me the cost of each of the many hunting trips they talked about. They were also aggressively friendly men, as Texans can be, full of crude language and dirty jokes, some of them funny. I liked them both.

It took more than an hour to hike across a brushy mountainside, up a steep willow draw, then alongside a small creek up a side draw. We were lucky. In the side draw, Luke found a covey almost at once. Ben and Robert each wanted a pair of quail to have mounted, with a couple of extra birds in case the taxidermist had a problem or made a mistake.

The Texans were decent shots, and twenty minutes after we'd found the covey, with six birds bagged, we were on our way back to my car. It's an understatement to say that Ben and Robert were elated. They high-fived each other, shouted, sang, jumped up and down, danced. They told me, over and over, how amazed and happy they were that my article hadn't been bullshit. And they kept offering to pay me, and I kept saying no.

Their return flight to Dallas wasn't scheduled until Sunday evening, but, when a rural tavern appeared alongside the road, they asked me to stop, and Robert used the pay phone to call the airline and change their reservations. By early afternoon, having spent about fourteen hours in southern Oregon, they were in the air on their way back to Dallas with six expensive mountain quail.

I remembered Tom Wolfe's novel *A Man in Full.* Protagonist Charlie Croker, owner of a Georgia quail plantation, announced to guests at a dinner party that, with all the expenses taken into account, the bobwhites they had been served cost him nearly five thousand dollars apiece.

Hunting quail wasn't the point with Charlie; talking about money was.

The Texans told me Charlie Croker stories during our hike across the mountainside back to the car. The previous year, Ben and Robert had gone on an extended African safari together, and when I asked them what they had shot, Robert answered simply and directly to the point. "It cost us over forty grand, because you pay by the animal, and we shot the shit out of everything," he said. "Forty fucking grand!"

When the talk turned back to birds, Ben explained that a quail grand slam was damned important, but their major bird-hunting goal was a "world slam" on turkeys for them both. They had already killed Rio Grandes in their home state, Eastern turkeys in Virginia, Merriams in South Dakota, and Osceolas in Florida. All that remained to complete their world slam were two Ocellated turkeys from the Yucatan Peninsula in Mexico.

Not long before coming to Oregon, Ben and Robert had traveled to the Yucatan, hired two local guides, and set off into what they described as a rain forest. The brothers didn't think it would matter much that they spoke no more than a few dozen words of Spanish, and that the guides spoke even less English. In any language, hunting was hunting, and they were men from Texas who could do the job.

After three days of heat, bugs, snakes, frustration, and futility, Ben came across a turkey, admittedly more through luck than skill. But he shot and killed it, and had his trophy, and all that remained was finding another turkey for Robert, and then getting both dead birds safely home.

Three more days failed to produce another Ocellated turkey. When their time ran out, with a single dead bird in hand, the hunters and guides began the long trek back out of the forest. Despite the language barrier, Ben was certain he had adequately stressed the importance of keeping his turkey in good condition for the taxidermist.

But camping overnight on the way out, the guides, off by themselves, roasted it over a fire for their dinner.

The brothers had already booked another trip to the Yucatan to try again. "It'll maybe end up costing as much as Africa," Robert said with a smile.

There were seven turkey vultures circling in the distance now. A plane crossed far behind them, leaving a white vapor trail across the blue sky. Scrub jays scolded from an oak limb over my head.

It occurred to me that of course Ben and Robert had been teenagers, too, probably not much different from Billy.

What happens to us?

$ $ $

I heard a strident screech and looked up to see a red-tail hawk soaring low in the sky, almost directly overhead, and just as the hawk sailed by and out of sight I heard quails calling.

I spotted a covey of California quail, a dozen or more birds in a tight group no more than twenty yards down the hill from my oak tree, busily pecking up weed seeds from a clearing in a patch of star thistle.

Once by me, the hawk must have flown a quick, tight circle. I looked back up just in time to see him stoop for the feeding birds. Wings laid back, the predator plummeted straight down, nearly too fast to see, and when he hit the ground the brown dust rose in a cloud and the quail burst into instantaneous flight, wings drumming as they scattered wildly in all directions.

No more than two or three seconds passed before the unsuccessful hawk had lifted back into flight and the quail had vanished into ground cover.

I watched the red-tail fly off eastward toward the mountains, high in the bright sky, soon becoming a dark speck, finally disappearing from view. Wherever the quail were, they remained silent, and the scrub jays had quieted too.

A log-truck down from the mountains, loaded with second-growth fir, sped along the two-lane road through our valley.

In the peace and silence after the log truck had gone, a clear, simple question came to mind, not for the first time:

Exactly what do you wish for Billy?

I wanted him to avoid extremes, to understand that big isn't necessarily better, and neither is more. I wanted him to recognize the differences, often vast, between what he had been conditioned to want and what he actually needed.

With that knowledge and lots of luck, he might find a constructive and gratifying way to live.

The old chestnut gelding that grazes the field where the quail had been feeding appeared at the wire fence a few yards away from where I sat. We were old friends, and he snorted and stamped a front hoof and then neighed, to make sure I knew he was there.

"Hey, *caballo*," I said. "*Como estas?*"

I got up and crossed the yard to the house, quartered an apple on the kitchen counter, and hurried back outside to feed him.

I liked the feel of his warm muzzle when, one after another, he gently lifted the apple pieces off the palm of my hand.

"Good stuff?" I asked him. "*Bueno?*"

All he did was chew.

$ $ $

Useful ideas often come when we have no reason to expect them. In my experience, one of the surest ways to answer a question or solve a problem is to quit thinking about it.

So it happened on a sunny Sunday morning when I drove to the Y to meet Billy for a shooting session. On an acre of fenced and irrigated pasture at a small farm about a mile from home, a young horse, a brown and white paint, was growing up. I enjoyed seeing him every time I drove the road to town. I'd been by the day he was born, a spindly-legged colt that could barely stand beside his mother, and now, six months later, at least half-grown, he was well-muscled and handsome, his coat lustrous in morning light. His mother remained in the pasture, but independence accompanies growth and strength, and the two horses were seldom side by side anymore.

Today, with the brown mare on the far side of the pasture and the colt close against the fence that bordered the road, I pulled onto the gravel shoulder and stopped with the window rolled down. Ears cocked forward, the colt looked up at me, switched his long black tail, and then lowered his head to bite off a mouthful of grass.

Across the pasture, a peacock sat perched atop the fence behind the mare, moving his head and neck and long tail as if to maintain balance. As the colt stood chewing grass, and once again looking at me, the bird flapped his wings and took off, flying low, skimming the grass, and dropped to a soft landing a few feet behind the colt. Immediately the peacock fanned his tail about halfway out, the long, delicate feathers glittering green and blue. Then he loosed a raucous call so loud that the colt jumped straight up, all four hoofs a foot or more off the ground.

An enjoyable show followed. When the colt landed, he wheeled around to face the peacock, and when the bird stepped forward, tail now fanned out all the way, the startled colt backed off. Then, ears laid back, he stepped tentatively toward the bird, which hopped backward and loosed another scream. With that, the colt came off the ground again, but this time when he landed, he lowered his head and charged at the strutting bird. Instead of taking flight, or backing off or running away, the peacock charged straight back at the colt and passed directly underneath him, right through the long black tail, and then, once out the other side, he pivoted quickly, his own formidable tail pressed against the fence, a few of the yard-long feathers poking out through the wire mesh.

When the colt turned to face the bird, the result was a brief Mexican standoff. The colt stood stiff-legged, tail switching, ears laid back, gazing at the peacock. The big bird stood there backed against the fence, neck stretched straight up, beady eyes staring back at the colt. This lasted ten or fifteen seconds.

Finally the colt appeared to lose interest and lowered his head to graze. With that, the peacock tilted his head to one side and stepped away from the fence to stand close beside the colt. Soon he produced another piercing call and ran off across the pasture, and the colt followed closely at a quick trot. When the peacock stopped, the colt did, too, then turned and trotted back the way he'd come. The peacock followed, close at his heels. The two of them played something like a game of tag, taking turns chasing each other around the pasture, circling and changing speeds, front to back and side to side. When I finally left, they were still happily at it.

Before I arrived at the Y, I thought I knew how I should talk to Billy from now until the time he left for Denver. Discrediting an irrational love of money remained necessary, but I knew it wouldn't be enough. I didn't merely want to call to Billy's attention the negatives that possessing a fortune sometimes brings. Whenever I could find a way, I had to stress the fact that the truly important essentials of a full life can surely be enjoyed without an excess of money.

I'd always kept a mental list of things to talk to my grandson about when reasonable opportunities presented themselves, a list that underwent continual revision as new ideas forced old ones out. Today, on the road between the pasture and the Y, I crossed out a remembrance of the Irish writer Oscar Wilde, even though one of his epigrams—I'd read it in college and never forgotten—suited my theme perfectly: *When I was young I thought that money was the most important thing in life; now that I am old, I know that it is.*

Wilde died in Paris at age forty-six, possibly of syphilis, not long after serving a two-year prison term resulting from a conviction involving male prostitutes. As a result of his legal difficulties, he died broke.

But why tell Billy that?

I also dropped an Ashland businessman from my list, one whose recent experiences demonstrate the truth of a Henry David Thoreau dictum—that people don't own things, but that things often own people. This gracious, friendly businessman operates motels throughout the west and had recently purchased one in Idaho, which contractors had extensively remodeled. Not long after the work was complete, meth addicts broke in late at night and trashed the place. Working to help clean up the mess, the owner strained his back and ended up hospitalized and in traction. Meanwhile, back home in Ashland, a drunken college girl snuck into one of his motels, also late at night, slipped on the tile deck of the swimming pool, split her head open, and subsequently filed a massive lawsuit against the motel.

But I realized there were better things to talk to a teenager about than the Oscar Wildes and Donald Trumps and unlucky businessmen of the world.

105th

I know that the very word (happiness) has come to have an odious ring, in America particularly. But there is no good reason why it should be thus. Happiness is as legitimate as sorrow, and everybody, except those emancipated souls who in their wisdom have found something better, or bigger, desires to be happy and would, if he could (if he only knew how!) sacrifice everything to attain it.

—Henry Miller, *The Rosy Crucifixion*

$ $ $

By the time I arrived at the Y on the morning of the paint horse and the peacock, these had become the entries at the top of my mental list:

I'd read a study concluding that the happiest people on earth lived in Costa Rica, the first of seven relatively poor

Central American and Caribbean countries ranked in the top ten on the list. America—the greatest and the richest country on Earth, as we're so often told—came in at 105th.

This didn't surprise me. After the Second World War, Costa Rica's progressive government disbanded its military and invested money in healthcare and education instead of bombs and guns. As neighboring countries logged their forests, Costa Rica preserved theirs by creating national parks that would soon attract multitudes of eco-tourists. Hilde and I visited the country twice, and in public buses and on crowded streets, on the beaches and in the parks, in local restaurants and neighborhood grocery stores, everywhere we went, we saw surprising numbers of people young and old exuding health, and school kids laughing, and parents showing love for their children—happy people indeed.

For a period of years, Hilde and I taught survival English to migrant workers, mostly Mexicans, in southern Oregon pear orchards. Our students ranged in age from teenagers to senior citizens. Despite putting in ten hours or more of grueling daily labor under a scorching sun before attending evening classes, they paid close attention, never complained about anything, and always had time for a beer with talk and laughter after class. In everything they said and did, they seemed substantially happier than the various orchard owners I'd met through the years.

Money Sucks

A few months after Hilde and I were married, while I was stationed at Fort Ord awaiting my army discharge, we found ourselves living in a small apartment two blocks above Fisherman's Wharf in Monterey. Hilde was pregnant. Our single room was so small that when we lowered the Murphy bed from the wall, we couldn't open the front door. Living prudently, we could afford one pizza a week, one movie a month, and the *San Francisco Chronicle* on Sundays. We owned a few books, a used radio, a small phonograph, and two records to play on it. We spent much of our free time hiking on nearby beaches. We were happy.

In the 1950s in Hawaii, the Waikiki beachboys were my heroes. Their names were enough to impress a boy from the mainland like me: Boat, Duke, Chick, Panama, Turkey, Rabbit, Buffalo, Splash, Blue. They worked the stretch of beach from the Royal Hawaiian Hotel down past the old Outrigger Canoe Club and Moana Hotel to the Waikiki Surf Club. They made their livings teaching surfing and taking tourists out to catch waves in eight-man koa wood canoes. In their ample free time, they surfed Queens and Canoes and speared fish and gathered lobsters and raced canoes and drank beer and played their ukuleles and talked story and sang their songs. They were doing what they wanted to do where they wanted to be with no apparent desire to possess more than they already had. Waikiki Beach was their self-contained world, and they knew and loved it. Statehood and jet planes and the business money that inevitably came along for the ride would quickly change their world, would soon destroy it, but when I knew them, they were the happiest people I'd ever seen.

I read a *Sports Illustrated* article about a young couple, both double-amputees, training to row in the 2012 Paralympics in London. The young man, an Iraq war veteran named Rob, is characterized this way: "What would he do with money anyway? He doesn't see the point of 'stuff that doesn't have a use . . . stuff you put up on a wall and display.' He travels with an acoustic guitar and an iPad, but not much else. He has two duffle bags of clothes but doesn't wear most of them. He thinks he might give most of his clothes away too.

"Rob lives on the $4,100 a month he gets from the Department of Veterans Affairs, and he enjoys living in hotels. When he and Oskana (his rowing partner) finished training in Orlando last winter, he went to the bank, cashed his monthly check, put it all inside a card he wrote out in Spanish using the Google Translator. Then he left the entire $4,100 for the cleaning woman at his hotel. He did not even know her name."

fist stick knife gun

Oh thou mighty and omnipotent, great and revered Almighty Dollar! Thou makest mankind corrupt and rotten! For thy smile, men commit murder, sacrifice every noble feeling, cut the throat of father, mother, brother or sister to gain thee. Men lose their hope of heaven.

—from the diary of Private Theodore Ewert, trumpeter of H Company in General George Armstrong Custer's expedition to the Black Hills of South Dakota in search of gold in 1874

$ $ $

From nine till eleven on Sunday mornings, the Y gym is reserved for adult men—they range in age from twenty-something to sixty-something—who choose up sides and compete in full-court pick-up basketball games. These folks play with all the aggressive drive, if not the skills, of high school and college players. With no disrespect intended, I think of them as the Weekend Warriors.

When Billy and I got there at five past eleven, they were still going at it, so, with the yells, grunts, groans, and curses of the warriors in the background—and the occasional heavy thud when one of them hit the floor hard—we sat and talked for a while: about fly fishing for trout and steelhead, the relative merits of marinated pork and beefsteak tacos, baseball in general, Derek Jeter's surprising season in particular, Steve Nash's signing with the Lakers, the rapper Eminem turning forty, skydiving, outdoor recreation in Colorado, and the Bill Maher movie *Religulous,* which Billy had heard about from a friend and wanted to see.

It was nearly half past eleven by the time we started shooting.

As tired, sweaty men straggled out the side door, Billy started with free throws.

"Taylor and Ethan argue about religion pretty often," he said.

Taylor, an atheist and the friend who had touted *Religulous,* and Ethan, a Baptist, were his baseball teammates.

"Chances are they both get at least some of their ideas from home," I answered. "They keep being friends, don't they?"

One after another, the free throws dropped cleanly through the net, and I caught the ball one-handed and bounced it back to the line.

"Ethan gets frustrated because Taylor usually wins the arguments."

"Bill Maher pretty much wins most of the arguments in his *Religulous* too. Do you get involved?"

"Mostly I listen."

"Good idea."

The last of the warriors, T-shirt draped over his pale shoulder, plastic water bottle in hand, disappeared through the door.

In the empty gym, Billy practiced all his shots, ending with his four consecutive three-pointers, four jumpers, and four free throws, then an extra-long shot from near midcourt, and finally a dunk.

After a drink at the water fountain, he ran a dozen "suicides," full-speed sprints up and down the length of the court. Last came a dribbling drill where he stood facing me from a few feet away and dribbled the ball with alternating hands while playing catch with me with a tennis ball with the off-hand.

We talked as he dribbled and caught and tossed the tennis ball.

"I got a book in the mail from Regis yesterday," he said, "to read before I get there."

"What kind of book?"

"*Fist Stick Knife Gun* is the title."

"Never heard of it. Non-fiction?"

"Non-fiction."

"What's it about?"

"I already read through a few chapters. The author's name is Canada. It's all about inner-city kids and gangs and violence."

"I get it," I said. "I think I do. Over the years things have progressed from fistfights to gunfights. It's true. When I was a kid, it was strictly fistfights. Not even sticks yet, never mind knives and guns. What class is it for?"

"Writing."

"Do you know when you leave yet?"

"Sometime a little after the middle of August. The 17th or 18th I think."

I was glad to hear about the book, but I didn't want to dwell on Billy leaving, so I told him about the steelhead Hilde had hooked and landed on our recent trip to the North Umpqua. The bright hen fish took a swinging wet fly inches beneath the surface near the head of the Tree Pool, jumped three feet out of water, landed with a loud splat, and then freight-trained downstream to the tail of the long pool, peeling off seventy or eighty yards of backing. Hilde stumbled over rocks and ledges to catch up, and as soon as she came close enough to tighten up the fly line, the steelhead jumped again and then ran through the rapids into the next downstream pool. Ten minutes later, I helped her land it there, a wild, thick fish fresh from the sea, the pink lateral line barely visible.

"I remember the one I hooked when we went," Billy said.

"We'll go again for sure before you leave."

Ten minutes of dribbling later, we headed for the hot tub, and had it to ourselves.

Billy asked me about the fishing trips Hilde and I had enjoyed in Baja back before he was born. I talked about it as we sat facing each other chest-deep in the warm, swirling water. I explained how I'd been writing for *Sports Illustrated* then, making money I'd never counted on, and instead of saving the extra money I'd taken the fall quarters off from teaching for several years. We always drove the 1,500 miles from Ashland to Loreto in October, on Interstate 5 all the way through California and then along Mexico's Route 1 the rest of the way. We stayed at a campground fifteen miles south of Loreto where spacious tents with bunk beds on concrete floors rented for three dollars a day. We moored our small aluminum boat half a mile down the road in Escondido Bay. Except for windy days, and they were rare, we set out every morning just before dawn, the sea flat as glass all the way to the offshore islands: Carmen, Coronado, and Danzante. We saw dolphins and whales, manta rays, flying fish, thresher sharks, vast schools of tuna feeding on the glassy surface while gulls, pelicans and frigate birds dove for showers of silver baitfish chased out of the water. With our streamer flies, we landed dorado, bonito, skipjack, yellowfin tuna, cabrilla, dog snapper, needlefish, sierra, rooster fish, and jack cravelle. We killed only enough for our dinners. On mornings when the fishing was too easy, we quit early and motored out to Ballantra Bay on Carmen Island to snorkel over rock ledges that teemed with fish. Our life was simple. Every few days, we drove to Loreto for long walks through town, and then shopped for mangoes, papayas, tortillas, Dos Equis beer, ice, and gasoline. On the way back to the campground, we stopped at our favorite bakery. To reach the ovens, we had to walk through a chicken coop, scattering hens and roosters. The pastries and rolls were fresh and delicious and the woman we paid totaled up our bill by writing numbers with her index finger on a breadboard dusted with flour. At the campground, we met people from all over America and from Europe and Japan, and we also came to know people who lived in town. The Mexicans we visited in town were poor and much like many Africans and Polynesians I'd known. They were nearly always smiling, clearly happy to be alive. Somewhere, somehow, they had discovered an important answer. Back from town at the campground in the late afternoons, with the Dos Equis stowed in the ice chest, we jogged a few miles south along the Baja highway and then back, and no beer ever tasted better than the two bottles we drank fresh from the ice chest after our runs. Drinking the cold Dos Equis, we sat outside and watched the bright sun set behind the steep wall of the Sierra de la Giganta Mountains. Occasional tarantulas showed themselves near the tent, and one night a desert fox came into the tent, but none of that did anything to diminish what were wonderful times. All I needed to keep my writing going was a few notebooks and a ballpoint pen. It was writing I believed in on significant environmental subjects, and, in *Sports Illustrated*, the articles reached a large audience that otherwise would almost surely never have known or had a chance to care about the issues. All Hilde needed to improve her impressive Spanish were natives to talk to and a dictionary. All we needed to be happy was what we had, what we did, and each other. I told Billy about it as best I could.

$ $ $

> If there is magic on this earth, it lies in water.
>
> —Loren Eiseley

ships and harbors

After the Y, we drove to La Tapatia for tacos.

Coming off the freeway at the Phoenix interchange, there was an elderly man leaning back against the guardrail beside the stop sign, holding a square of cardboard bearing a neatly printed message:

UNEMPLOYED VETERAN
NEED FOOD
ANYTHING HELPS

He had an unkempt gray beard and wore a John Deere cap, a black T-shirt, threadbare khaki pants, and muddy boots. As I lowered the window with my left hand and fumbled two dollar bills out of my wallet with my right, he climbed to his feet and stepped up to the car.

"Thank you, sir, God bless," he said as he took the money, and he smiled and nodded, his dark eyes glittering under the bill of the cap. "God bless you, man," he said again.

"Good luck to you," I answered as he turned away.

When the driver behind me honked his horn, I made it a point to wait a few extra seconds before pulling away, slowly.

"I wonder what he'll buy," Billy said.

"It doesn't matter to me. He's about the right age to be a Vietnam vet. If he is one, he shouldn't have to sit there begging. No matter what he is, he shouldn't have to be out there doing that."

When we ordered at La Tapatia, I asked the young woman behind the counter about the taco challenge, and she told us that nobody had finished thirty tacos in thirty minutes yet.

"I doubt if anybody ever will," I said to Billy. "I'd bet against it."

"What about Joey Chestnut though?"

"But he stuffs those hot dogs down his throat, he doesn't even swallow. You can't get a taco down that way."

"Maybe not. But I wouldn't mind seeing him try."

The television set was tuned into a cable news channel again, possibly because of the ongoing presidential campaign. But I didn't use the opportunity to insult Republicans or greed freaks. Something in me had changed.

Once, when we were about halfway through our meal, a Mitt Romney campaign ad appeared on the screen, featuring the candidate himself.

"What do you think of him?" Billy asked me.

In the space of a couple of seconds, a dozen or more possible answers raced through my mind, all of them insulting. I had to say something, so I chose the least offensive response that had occurred to me. "Just judging from his looks and the way he's come across lately, I think he might have a future in erectile dysfunction commercials."

When our tacos arrived, we both had sense enough to ignore the television.

A Mexican family took the table next to ours, a husband and wife with two lovely pre teen daughters, all of them dressed as if they'd been to mass.

As we ate, Billy asked if I'd watched an ESPN program about wealthy professional athletes going broke after retirement.

"I remember I saw a commercial about it," I said, "but I didn't watch the show. I think I know what usually happens though. I've read some stuff on the subject. Swindlers and conmen love to take advantage of naïve young people with lots of money. They get them roped into bad investments and business deals. Producing useless products. Buying worthless land. Even making religious movies that hardly anybody ever sees. Bill Maher should've put that in

Religulous. One sad thing about those athletes losing their money is that they already had more than enough to begin with. What retired athletes really need is something that makes sense to do with the rest of their lives."

The older of the daughters at the next table pointed up at the television set, and her sister looked and they laughed together happily, so I looked too.

"Hey," I told Billy. "Somebody turned Bugs Bunny on."

$ $ $

The time until Billy left for Denver and Regis went well.

The school mailed him another required text, a book titled *The Immortal Life of Henrietta Lacks*.

We shot baskets together nearly every day. Occasionally, either while we shot or over tacos afterward, I talked to him, calmly and briefly, about why people want more money than they need and what getting it often does to them. We spent most of our time on other subjects: books, music, movies, mountains, rivers, birds, fish, the Yankees, water sports, Texas hold 'em poker. I kept in mind simple words of wisdom I'd often heard from my Hawaiian beachboy friends as a boy: *Cool head main t'ing*.

I checked the Henrietta Lacks book out of our university library and read it along with Billy, and I was impressed with Regis for assigning it to their freshmen. The title character, a poor southern tobacco farmer, has the cancer cells that killed her alive today in cultures all over the world, cells that were largely responsible for the polio vaccine, important cancer research, cloning, and in vitro fertilization. The cells that came from Henrietta Lacks have been bought and sold by the hundreds of billions, yet sixty years after her death, she lies buried in an unmarked grave. No one in her family has ever been compensated for her incalculable contributions to medical research.

I also read *Fist Stick Knife Gun* and was happier than ever with Regis. Geoffrey Canada writes honestly and therefore compellingly about the inevitable prevalence of violence among young people growing up in ghettos. Included is a powerful indictment of the twelve-billion-dollar gun industry that designs and manufactures weapons expressly designed to appeal to juveniles.

Not long after I finished Canada's book, a young man named James Holmes entered a movie theater premiering a Batman film—*The Dark Knight Rises*—in Aurora, Colorado, a suburb of Denver. Holmes was armed with a Glock handgun, a Remington tactical shotgun, and a semi-automatic rifle with a 100-round magazine. After throwing a teargas canister, he opened fire on the mostly young audience, murdering twelve people and wounding fifty-eight.

When he was younger, Billy had been something of a Batman fan, and before long he would be in Denver, so we talked about the Aurora murders, killings that could have happened in Ashland or any other American town. Soon enough, another massacre would follow. Just as surely, Republicans and the NRA will continue to issue their standard arguments on behalf of the sanctity of guns.

$ $ $

The night before he left for Denver, Billy drove out to say goodbye. It was a pleasant Oregon August evening, cooling off quickly after sunset on a hot day.

Hilde and I weren't looking forward to this, and when Billy walked through the front door, I saw that he wasn't either.

We sat out on our deck, where Hilde and I spend most of our time nearly every evening from spring through fall. The turkey vultures had already gone to roost, and honking flocks of geese flew overhead on their way to Emigrant Lake for the night. Mallards circled to land in the pond at the bottom of the hill.

Hilde and I sat at the table with glasses of wine and Billy had ice water.

We began by making small talk—about the weather in Colorado in wintertime, about how the Ashland High

School basketball and baseball teams would likely do in the coming year.

We talked about the final two-part episode of *House*, and about how Billy's thirteen-year-old brother, Jake, had been growing lately, seemingly about an inch per month.

Before signing his commitment letter to Regis, Billy had made a three-day visit to the school, and he answered some questions I had about the coaching staff and the campus.

For a minute or two, we were silent.

It had grown dark enough while we talked for the first stars to appear in the eastern sky.

In the silence, one hen mallard quacked down on the pond.

"I said goodbye to a lot of people today," Billy said. "This is the hardest."

Then all three of us were weeping.

Finally, we all knew he would really leave in the morning, for Denver and the wide world, and it took us a long time to say goodbye.

$ $ $

Hilde and I talked things over after Billy had gone. We agreed that he had to establish his own values and beliefs, had to create an independent life of his own. If we had helped in the process so far, and I hoped and believed we had, much of it had happened naturally and imperceptibly.

What we said during the summer before he left home for college mattered, but how we had lived together as husband and wife and related to our grandson over eighteen years had undoubtedly mattered more.

$ $ $

A ship is safe in harbor but that is not what ships are for.
—Graham Mackintosh, *Into a Desert Place*

3

other places, other selves

He who knows he has enough is rich.

—Tao Te Ching

To be able to work at and for what one most wants to do well, should be gospel in our democracy.

—Frank Lloyd Wright

voyaging

On a drive to town on a sunny October afternoon, I saw that the handsome paint colt was gone from his pasture, possibly sold. His dam grazed alone, cropping grass close against the fence that bordered the road, and there was no sign of a peacock anywhere.

A week later, the colt still absent, sold for sure, I took an early morning flight from Medford to Denver to visit Billy. I had no idea what to expect. During the two months since he'd left, we'd kept in touch regularly with texts and phone calls, and he'd told me more than once that he liked the school, that his classes were going well, and that basketball was off to a good start. But, predictably enough, he sometimes sounded homesick.

Hilde dropped me off at the Medford Airport 4:45 a.m.

For the next half hour, as I suffered the standard humiliations inflicted on air travelers, lines from a Henry Miller essay stayed lodged in my mind: *Flying is the lowest form of voyaging. One might as well be a lump of shit.* I wondered how bleakly Miller might have described air travel had he lived to see the twenty-first century.

After passing through the final security checkpoint with my carry-on bag, my only luggage, I found an uncomfortable plastic seat in the stuffy waiting room, thinking I'd kill the forty-five minutes until boarding time watching TV. But the airport sets were tuned to Fox News, what I judged to be a re run of a panel show consisting of female blonds and male geeks.

I got up and carried my bag back and forth across the waiting room and spent the time daydreaming instead. I recalled the last time I'd been in Colorado, anywhere other than the Denver airport, more than fifty years ago. When I left Denver that time, hitchhiking with a friend, a state trooper pulled up around midnight on a lonely highway somewhere east of the city. The trooper climbed out of his car slowly, as if it needed considerable effort, then strolled nonchalantly up to us, gravel crunching under his boots. With a smile on his pale face, he informed us that hitchhiking was illegal in Colorado, and if we didn't start walking immediately, and keep walking, he'd arrest us and take us in. We had no choice but to start off eastward along the shoulder of the road, taking turns shouldering our crammed-full, heavy duffle bag. For five or six hours, the trooper cruised back and forth, east and west, checking on us. Once he yelled out his window as he passed slowly by: "Hey, assholes, pick up the pace!" We didn't pick up the pace, but we kept moving, and by sunrise, after we'd walked probably twenty miles, he finally gave up—maybe his shift was over—and soon after he disappeared, we caught a ride with a trucker all the way into Kansas.

After I'd traversed the waiting room eighty or ninety times, the flight was announced, and we boarded the small United Airlines plane. I had a window seat in the third row from the front. Once, flying from Denver to Rapid City, South Dakota, on a writing assignment, I'd had the identical seat assignment in the same-sized plane, and soon after I'd settled into my seat for that flight, a friendly, smiling man took the aisle seat beside me. He weighed at least five hundred pounds and kept me squashed and flattened against the wall of the plane for two hours. I'm fairly claustrophobic to begin with, and if he hadn't been such a nice guy—he talked knowledgably about the Lakota Sioux Indians and the Pine Ridge Reservation—I might have begged the flight attendant for a parachute.

Today my luck was better. The man who sat next to me had a book of Gore Vidal essays with him. He turned out to be a retired United pilot who owned and ran a winery in the Applegate Valley and was now on the first leg of a trip to France to meet with other vintners.

With the plane barely lifted off the runway, with no encouragement from me, my seatmate initiated a conversation about money. Frustrated with the political scene and with greed-freaks in general, he had searched out a study on the relationship between income and what people normally define as happiness. The study he came up with—he was convinced it was legitimate—concluded that, in America, nothing above a yearly income of $75,000 appeared to have any appreciable effect on happiness or general well-being.

After that, we talked about other things—food, wine, football, flying planes, surfing—all the way to Denver.

Into our descent, the early morning sunlight showed a hazy shroud of smog against the snowcapped Rocky Mountains.

The Denver airport, twenty-five miles outside the city, in the proverbial middle of nowhere, covers fifty-three square miles, the largest airport in America and the second largest on Earth, after the King Fahd International Airport in Saudi Arabia. My strong impression about the place was that it contributed further proof, if any was required, that the way we live much of our lives is insane.

The biggest airport in America is comprised of escalators, lengthy hallways, subway trains, and gigantic waiting rooms furnished with sterile furniture and fixtures. Hardly anything as real as wood, leather, or stone can be found anywhere. Long lines of compliant people slowly snake their way through security checkpoints, behaving as submissively as herds of cattle in feedlots. All of them—the tattooed motorcyclists in Harley-Davidson jackets, the businessmen with neckties, the businesswomen in tailored suits, the college students, the grandparents, the young moms and dads with children, the men who look like preachers, the men who look like pimps, the disabled, the morbidly obese, the anorexic—take off their shoes, empty their pockets into plastic containers, are screened by metal detectors, and pose in front of body scanning machines as if rehearsing for their crucifixions. The hallways are lined with shops offering goods nobody needs along with the standard assortment of restaurants and bars that sell over-priced food and drink to people bored enough to pay the inflated prices, just to have something, anything, to do. Everywhere there were people sitting, standing, walking, lying down, staggering drunkenly, many staring transfixed—yes, even including some of the drunks—at the screens of their wireless technology.

After a long walk through crowded hallways, an underground train ride, then another long walk through more crowded hallways, I found an information counter where a friendly man gave me directions to a booth that offered a shuttle service to town. I followed his directions but got lost twice before I found the booth, where I paid another friendly man fifty dollars for the twenty-five mile ride to the Motel 6 where I had reservations—a motel I'd chosen because it was cheap and less than half a mile from the Regis campus.

This second friendly man handed me my shuttle ticket and, not so friendly anymore, impatiently explained how to reach the "island" outside where Van number 14 would pick me up at 10:15; but I got lost again before I finally found my way outside. Luckily, I made it to the "island" in time to catch Van 14, which took me to Denver with seven other airport refugees: two young men and a young woman who looked to be students, two businessmen working on their pods, or pads, or whatever they were, and a radiant mother with a baby girl sucking on a pacifier.

Sunlight shimmered off thousands upon thousands of cars parked in neat rows in the vast lots adjacent to the airport. Far beyond the parking lots, I saw silver planes landing and taking off. The freeway, I-70, was clogged with cars, buses, vans, pickups, and semi-trucks. I wished that somehow it could be made possible to momentarily stop all the planes and motor vehicles, just long enough to learn where everyone was coming from and where they were going and why, and then to calculate how much of it made any actual sense.

After forty-five minutes of these and other idle thoughts, I was the first passenger out of the van.

As I checked into the motel, just off the freeway, I asked the woman behind the desk for directions to Regis. She assured me I couldn't miss it—straight up the residential street across from the parking lot, then a left-turn at the end of the street, and there it would be.

My third floor room was what I'd expected, clean and adequate, with a bed, a table, two chairs, a small dresser, a television set, and a bathroom the size of a broom closet. Most importantly, with the outside door closed, I could barely hear the freeway.

I called Hilde to talk and let her know I'd arrived, and then I texted Billy, asking him to text me back when he could.

I washed, changed clothes, and started off for Regis.

Before I was halfway across the parking lot Billy answered, asking me to let him know when I arrived on campus and tell him exactly where I was, and he'd come and meet me.

The quiet residential street led through a working class neighborhood with small, well-kept houses, and ended at four-lane Regis Boulevard, where, off to my left, was the school. First I walked by well-tended green athletic fields, and just beyond them came the classroom buildings and dormitories.

I've seen a lot of lovely campuses in Europe and across America, including our Ivy League schools, and Regis seemed as beautiful as any of them. The trees in their vivid fall colors helped create the impression, and so did the stately red brick buildings, the many outdoor benches and tables, the old trees and grassy lawns, and the neat compactness of it all.

Outside a building named Carroll Hall, I sat on a stone bench set between a spruce tree and a hardwood and texted Billy again, who answered at once and said he was on his way.

While I waited, a few students wandered by, all of them looking happy on a fine fall day. All around me, red squirrels busily scampered back and forth across the lawn and up and down the trees.

"Hey, Opa!"

He'd come up from behind me.

When I turned and saw Billy, I knew at first glance that his life was going well, that he was confident and happy.

We embraced.

"It's so good to see you!" I said.

"Good to see you, Opa!"

I was happy too.

$ $ $

It was lunchtime on Thursday when we first met outside Carroll Hall, and I would leave Denver Monday afternoon. That gave us a long weekend that seemed too short when it ended.

Billy's roommate was a point-guard named Kevin from Wilsonville, Oregon. As dorm rooms go, theirs was spacious and something approaching almost neat, with a picture window offering a pleasing view of green lawns and fall foliage.

On Thursday night in the dorm lounge, Billy and I talked about school as we watched the Oregon Ducks beat Arizona State. He told me that his writing teacher had already graded papers on *The Immortal Life of Henrietta Lacks* and *Fist Stick Knife Gun*, and his current writing assignment dealt with a book I knew fairly well, Jonathan Kozol's *Amazing Grace*. Kozol's narrative presents the challenges faced by poor children in urban America and highlights the strength and dignity that they often exhibit in coming to terms with their difficult lives. Along with all this, Billy was also reading Aristotle.

Back at the motel after the game, I called Hilde to talk and tell her about our grandson, how he seemed different already, no less friendly and considerate than ever, but more sure of himself, more independent. Three weeks before his nineteenth birthday, he'd established a new life a thousand miles from home, and he liked it.

As I got ready for bed, I turned the television on, and what appeared on the screen might have been the Travel Channel profiling exclusive resorts where Russian oligarchs spend their leisure time, or a *Saturday Night Live* sketch. Elderly white men with paunches and jowls lounged in the shade of palm trees beside a turquoise swimming pool. Next to each of the malformed men sat an attractive woman in a scant bikini decades younger than her escort. The old men and young women were eating hors d'oeuvres from silver trays and sipping drinks from tall, frosted glasses, everything served by obsequious dark-skinned men wearing immaculate white jackets. In the bright sunlight beyond the palms, the vast sea lay flat and blue beneath a cloudless sky.

It had been a good day all around, so none of it disgusted me or made me angry. My mood was so good that I laughed at the scene.

$ $ $

On Friday, Billy and I sat on a bench in the warm shade under an oak tree to talk about his writing assignment. I suggested he quote both Mitt Romney's infamous "47 percent speech" and Barbara Ehrenreich's review of *Amazing Grace* in his paper. Romney's cruel mindset helped create the urban ghettos Kozol wrote about. In contrast, Ehrenreich called the young people who live in Kozol's ghettos "children of intelligence and humor, of poetic insight and luminous faith."

Outside of class, all Regis students perform community service, and Billy and Kevin had volunteered to teach math to ex-convicts who hoped to either return to school or pass high school equivalency tests. Mention of the volunteer work and how it related to *Amazing Grace* was to be included in the paper.

Late Friday afternoon we watched a Regis soccer game that the home team won, 4–2.

We ate at a place Billy knew, a small pizza parlor just off campus run by an elderly black man and apparently staffed by his family.

After the pizza, we shot pool in the Student Union.

I met Billy's coaches, watched a Saturday morning practice, and saw for myself what I'd already known: Billy could play successfully at the college level.

While Billy did homework through the afternoon, I walked across the bridge over I-70 to Rocky Mountain Lake Park. I jogged around the lake three times, through feeding flocks of Canada geese, and then took a long walk through the neighborhood beyond the park. Here the houses were large and often ornate, with groomed lawns and carefully tended shrubs and trees. But the region seemed all but dead—no bicycles or toys in any of the yards, or any other signs of children, nobody doing yard work, nobody walking the quiet streets. Before I'd gone far, I turned and went back to the park, where the Canada geese would keep me company.

Later that afternoon, I walked from the motel to Regis and saw children shooting baskets, playing catch, and jumping rope in the undersized yards of the little houses. Dogs barked behind wire fences in some of the yards, and adults worked on cars in driveways and sat talking on porches. Families actually lived here.

Billy and I caught a bus for downtown Denver at a stop just off campus on Regis Boulevard. Our plan was to take a walk through town and eventually find a P. F. Chang's restaurant for a Chinese dinner. We took seats near the front of the bus, and for the first few minutes, the ride was uneventful. Then at a stop near a busy intersection, a young couple climbed aboard with their clothing in tatters and their faces smeared with blood.

Several passengers were understandably startled at the sight, and the driver stood to peer outside, presumably to see what might have happened. Traffic accident? Gang violence? Riot? I looked too, but saw nothing unusual anywhere.

"Don't worry," the bloody young man said as he paid his fare. "We're okay. This is just for fun."

He and his female companion found seats near the middle of the bus. I couldn't keep myself from glancing at them from time to time, and they appeared to be engaged in normal conversation.

When we stepped off the bus not far from Coors Field, we saw bloody people everywhere: men, women, and children with gashes in bare arms and legs, with punctured throats, with eyes dangling from sockets, with daggers and cleavers and hatchets through their heads.

Billy asked a pony-tailed man wearing a blood-soaked white shirt, and with a wooden-handled butcher knife protruding from his chest, if all of this had anything to do with the television show *The Walking Dead*.

The man drew us aside and, standing against the wall of a building, he explained. Organized by the city of Denver, this was the Zombie Crawl, purportedly the largest gathering of zombies in the history of the world. Many events were scheduled through the day and well into the night, and participants had been urged to bring along non-perishable food items to donate to the Food Bank of the Rockies.

We walked among the zombies for an hour or more in the general area of the Sixteenth Street Mall. There had to be tens of thousands of them. They came in all ages, shapes, and sizes and displayed a remarkable variety of wounds, deformities, and gore. Billy asked a passerby to take our picture, then handed the man his cell phone, and we posed against a building with a splendid zombie standing between us, a heavy bald man in a tattered suit with his face painted white, a screwdriver stuck through the side of his skull, and bright red blood leaking from the entry wound and the corners of his mouth.

The Chinese food at P. F. Chang's was excellent, but an odd thing about the place was that no Asians seemed to work there. I ordered the first martini I'd had in years. While sitting at the window table sipping gin and vermouth, and from our appetizers through our beef and shrimp, I watched the zombies walking, lurching and staggering in both directions along the sidewalks and up and down the street.

The martini tasted so good that I ordered another.

Over dessert, a vision that was likely induced by a combination of gin and my love of political satire came to mind. If the month had been August instead of October, and with the addition of a few palm trees, the Zombie Crawl could have passed for the Republican National Convention in Tampa, Florida. Their presidential candidate, at the head of the pack of walking dead, could totter along as always, legs stiff, torso tense, like an old man afraid of slipping and falling on ice.

But I told none of this to Billy, because I didn't think it was necessary. I felt certain that Mitt Romney couldn't be elected president. What mattered more to me than an irrelevant presidential candidate was the fact that during dinner, Billy and I had talked about politics, sports, his teachers, his first-semester classes, his new friends, his past experiences, and a few of his future dreams. He was reading and understanding books that dealt with the thoroughly decent concept of helping people who needed it. He had recently become friends with a Hispanic ex-convict he tutored in math in his Service Learning class. For his second semester of Service Learning, he would work in a Denver homeless shelter.

Despite our complicated and volatile world, Billy seemed secure in his burgeoning life.

$ $ $

On Sunday, my last full day in Denver, we ate burritos for lunch at the Regis cafeteria and then walked across campus to the field house to shoot baskets. The fall colors seemed lovelier than ever, and the red squirrels were out in force.

About halfway to the field house, Billy called to a young woman passing by and asked her to take our picture, this time on the spacious lawn in front of Main Hall, the administration building where President Clinton and Pope John had posed together twenty years ago.

Entering through a side door, we found the field house deserted and crossed the shiny floor between tiers of empty seats.

In the locker room as Billy changed, I grabbed a ball from the bin, and then we walked back out to the court.

I'd always loved shooting with him, and I'd missed it, and we fell easily into our old habits.

He began with short set shots, then mid-range jumpers, then three-pointers, hitting nearly everything.

"Your shot seems as good as ever," I said.

He stepped to the free-throw line.

"We practice really hard, lots of drills, and we run lots of suicides, and for a while my legs were so wiped out, my shot was off, but I'm okay now."

"Yes you are."

"I'm glad I ran some through the summer. When the team did two-mile runs, I came in third or fourth."

He drained one three-pointer after another.

"I'm really happy that you like it here," I said.

"I do like it."

"I could tell you were happy as soon as I saw you. But do you hear kids complaining much? I mean, college kids usually do. About the food, for instance."

"Not so much the food. But I definitely miss La Tapatia tacos. I hear some complaints about the lame party scene."

"The party scene?"

"Oh yeah."

"I guess things haven't changed a hell of a lot in more than half a century. Did we ever watch *Animal House*?"

"Remember? We watched it at your house."

"How's your fantasy football team?"

"Not so hot. I couldn't draft Peyton Manning for quarterback so I ended up with Michael Vick and he's inconsistent and always gets hurt. Too bad the Broncos have a bye today. We could've watched together."

After a long string of made free throws, Billy finally bounced one off the back rim.

"Want to shoot?" he asked me.

"Sure, I'll try a few."

He passed me the ball.

"There's quite a few rich kids here," he said.

"There'd have to be. It's an expensive school."

I stood at the line, dribbled twice, shot, and missed.

"They have lots of expensive stuff. I don't think stuff matters so much. Experiences do."

After three straight misses, I made five straight and stepped from the line. "I'll quit when I'm a little ways ahead," I said. "By the way, both your coaches told me you'd be getting plenty of minutes. As a freshman, you might not start, but that's okay, just so you play."

"I forgot to tell you I already talked to the baseball coach and met with the team. I guess I'll red shirt this year in baseball and then next season they'll turn me into an outfielder."

"Sounds good. You can totally concentrate on basketball for now. I'm really glad we got to shoot together here."

"Me too!"

Billy shot three-pointers, then jumpers, then free throws again, then made his standard finishing routine look easy. Between shots, he told me about a girl he'd met.

In the late afternoon, he worked on his Kozol paper in his room while I hung out at the motel, first reading and then watching football.

When I called Hilde, I told her I was more convinced than ever that Billy was at a good place; that he was taking school work more seriously than I had at his age; that he'd mentioned a pretty blonde cross-country runner, and not ten minutes later I'd seen her—it couldn't have been anybody else—running down Regis Boulevard as I walked toward the motel; and that I knew for certain he was satisfied with life.

We watched Sunday night football, the Steelers and Bengals, in the dorm lounge. A week later, the Broncos and Saints would play on Sunday night, and I agreed with Billy that Peyton Manning, back after a year off due to injury, was still the best quarterback in the NFL.

After the game—the Steelers won, 24–17—Billy walked with me across campus. It was a clear, starry night, the air fresh and cool, and students strolled leisurely along the walkways between the lighted buildings.

"When's your last class over tomorrow?"

"I'll get out a little after eleven."

"I'll come over and meet you and say goodbye."

"I'm glad you came, Opa."

"I am too. We all miss you. But you're happy here so I am too. We all are."

"I'll get to come home eight days for Christmas."

"We can shoot every day if you want."

"A few times maybe we can go to La Tapatia afterward."

"Maybe you can try for thirty tacos in thirty minutes."

"Maybe not thirty. But at least ten."

We arrived at the gate that led out to Regis Boulevard, with four lanes of traffic moving through the night.

As we stood by the gate, a nearly empty bus rolled by.

"I can walk with you all the way to your room," Billy said.

"I'll make it all right. This looks like a pretty safe neighborhood. Anyway, I can still run some. I guess I could even fight some if I had to."

"Night, Opa."

"Goodnight, buddy."

"Goodnight."

Once outside the gate, I turned and looked back and watched him striding away, tall and strong, in his new home where he had made it.

$ $ $

> One day their childhood, and your enjoyment of it, was over. They take off as strangers, not confessing who they presently are. You tried to stay close, in touch, but they were other selves in other places.
>
> —Bernard Malamud, *Dubin's Lives*

politics, film, and coffee

It's true that when I was growing up, there was a sort of division: respect was accorded to people who made great movies and to people who made movies that made a lot of money. And that division just doesn't exist anymore: Now it's just the people who make a lot of money . . . It's become horrible the way people with money decide they can fart in the kitchen.

—Stephen Soderbergh, film maker

$ $ $

Saying goodbye the next morning was easier than it had been the last time, the night before Billy left Ashland. The boy I'd known and loved had become a young man.

The shuttle van picked me up in front of the motel a little after noon. I was the last one aboard. Except for a middle-aged woman accompanied by a sullen teenage boy with a tattooed neck, my fellow passengers were businessmen carrying laptops. The teenager sat directly in front of me, so I leaned far enough forward to decipher enough to know that the neck tattoos were bible verses.

Back on the freeway, with the driver taking the fast lane all the way, I pondered Billy's future. There was no way to begin to know what would eventually happen in his life. He might major in math, or philosophy, or both. He might decide to teach and coach after college. He might become a doctor or a lawyer. He might go into business, which will be fine if he that's what he really wants—maybe a taco restaurant modeled after La Tapatia. He might become a sports agent, like Dave Stewart. In six months or a year or two, he might fall in love with a cross-country runner—or a waitress or nurse or nun willing to leave her order—and decide to marry. And he might do any number of other things I can't begin to imagine.

Whatever he does, I believe he'll see through and well beyond the allure of making as much money as possible. Of course, he'll need a certain income, something close to average, or a little more. Unless the greed freaks manage to bring us down even sooner than anyone predicts, he might be lucky enough to find his happiness doing something real, something that matters, in a place he wants to be.

Blind luck will surely play a major role in Billy's life, as it does with everybody. Though some people hate to admit it, much of what happens to us is rooted in a capricious blend of chance and chaos. Insofar as I could, I've tried to do my best for Billy, and when he's back in southern Oregon we'll continue to hang out together, shoot baskets, fly fish, enjoy tacos at La Tapatia, and talk about just about everything. I love him and care, with the understanding that things that come from the heart can never be fully understood or explained.

After the shuttle van, it was back into the second biggest airport on Earth.

My two-and-a-half hours of waiting consisted, as usual, of brief periods of petty humiliation and longer periods of boredom.

After I'd complied with the written directions, my ticket was issued out of a machine—no human contact whatsoever at the airline counter. With my carry-on strap over my shoulder, I walked a good three miles up and down the long corridors, crowded with the typical motley crew of people hurrying along in both directions.

I saw a contingent of young soldiers in fatigues waiting in line to board their plane. They looked like teenagers to me, and I remembered a poem I'd read long ago in college that compared soldiers to innocent lambs being herded into a slaughterhouse.

After I'd done my walking, I located the gate where my flight was scheduled to depart. With more than an hour to wait, the area wasn't crowded yet. I took a plastic chair with a discarded newspaper on it, only a few yards from a coffee stand and facing a window looking out across the runways.

I skimmed through the paper.

The number one box office movie for the previous week had been something titled "Taken 2," an "action thriller" about killing people, sequel to an earlier action thriller about killing people. It had earned $49,522,194.

On the sports page, I read an article about one of Billy's early basketball heroes, Allen Iverson. Iverson had earned about $150 million during his playing career, but now, a few years after retirement, he was quickly going broke. At present, he had $62,000 per month coming into his bank account and $360,000 going out. He owed various creditors $125,750 per month. His monthly expenses included $1,000 for dry cleaning, $10,000 for new clothes, and another $10,000 on restaurants. His mansion in Atlanta was in foreclosure.

Another sports page story dealt with the Penn State child abuse scandal. The university's hierarchy, esteemed Coach Joe Paterno included, had subverted the truth for years, and the principal motivating factor had been the tens of millions of dollars donated to Penn State thanks to football.

On the editorial page was a column estimating the sums likely to be spent during the 2012 election campaigns. The presidential candidates would go through more than a billion dollars apiece, mostly collected from rich men and mostly spent on television ads. State and local candidates would spend around four billion dollars more, and at every level the candidates with the most money would almost always win.

When I looked up from the paper, I saw a mother and daughter stow their flight bags underneath a table near the coffee stand. The mother, an attractive woman, wore coal-black slacks and a gold-colored blouse, and her shoulder-length hair exactly matched the color and sheen of the slacks. She smiled at her daughter lovingly and then went to the counter to order for them. The daughter, nine or ten years old, looked like her mother—hair, eyes, immaculate complexion, everything. Waiting at the table, she gazed out the window at the runways.

I've always admired mothers and children who seem happy together. These two at the airport reminded me of a mother and daughter who took seats directly across from Hilde and me on a public bus traveling from San Jose, Costa Rica, to Manuel Antonio on the Pacific coast. The Costa Rican mother, wearing jeans and a gold-colored blouse, was a very beautiful woman, yet it seemed apparent that her beauty meant little if anything to her, that she cared more about her daughter than anything or anybody else on Earth. The two of them talked and laughed together virtually nonstop for more than three hours, and seeing them and listening to them made the trip in the stuffy bus a joy.

The airport mother returned to the table with two tall paper cups. She and her daughter sipped their drinks and talked for a little while, and then the mother took her cell phone out, and the daughter went back to staring out the window.

I went back to my paper. I scanned articles about Wall Street thieves, corrupt judges, environmental disasters, drug busts, politicians denying the science of climate change for the sake of profits, Middle East wars, and American murders.

After half an hour, I looked up just as the mother and daughter left. When they were halfway out to the nearest hallway, they stopped, and the daughter hurried back to the table, where she'd forgotten her flight bag. I watched her pick the bag off the floor and then look furtively back at her mother, who by then was reading a monitor showing flight information. The daughter quickly reached out and stole the tip—two or three dollars—that her mother had left on the table. She crumpled the bills up and stuffed them into her pocket, and, smiling now, flight bag in hand, she walked away.

Not enough money sucks. Too much money sucks. Which is to say, money sucks. Yes, it really does.

Money Sucks

$ $ $

I feel more and more that we must not judge God on the basis of this world; it's a study that didn't come off. What can you do, in a study that has gone wrong, if you are fond of the artist? You do not find much to criticize; you hold your tongue. But you have a right to ask for something better. This life of ours, so much criticized, and for such good and even exalted reasons—we must not take it for anything but what it is, and go on hoping that in some other life we'll see a better thing than this.

—Vincent Van Gogh, in a letter to his brother Theo